SUBJECT RETRIEVAL
IN THE SEVENTIES

CONTRIBUTIONS IN LIBRARIANSHIP AND
INFORMATION SCIENCE

Series Editor: Paul Wasserman

SUBJECT RETRIEVAL IN THE SEVENTIES

NEW DIRECTIONS

PROCEEDINGS OF AN
INTERNATIONAL SYMPOSIUM
HELD AT THE
CENTER OF ADULT EDUCATION
UNIVERSITY OF MARYLAND
COLLEGE PARK
MAY 14 TO 15, 1971

EDITED BY
HANS (HANAN) WELLISCH
AND
THOMAS D. WILSON

CONTRIBUTIONS IN LIBRARIANSHIP AND INFORMATION SCIENCE
NUMBER 3

GREENWOOD PUBLISHING COMPANY
WESTPORT, CONNECTICUT

PUBLISHED IN CONJUNCTION WITH THE
SCHOOL OF LIBRARY AND INFORMATION SERVICES
UNIVERSITY OF MARYLAND

1972

Library of Congress Cataloging in Publication Data
Main entry under title:

Subject retrieval in the seventies.

(Contributions in librarianship and information
science, no. 3)
"Proceedings of an international symposium held at
the Center of Adult Education, University of Maryland,
College Park, May 14 to 15, 1971."
Includes bibliographies.
1. Subject headings--Congresses. 2. Classifica-
tion--Books--Congresses. 3. Information storage
and retrieval systems--Congresses. I. Wellisch,
Hanan, ed. II. Wilson, Thomas D., ed. III. Maryland. University. Center of Adult Education.
IV. Series

Z695.S89   025.3'3   70-183149
ISBN 0-8371-6322-6

Library of Congress Catalog Card Number: 70-183149
ISBN: 0-8371-6322-6

Greenwood Publishing Company
A Division of Greenwood Press, Inc.
51 Riverside Avenue, Westport, Connecticut 06880
School of Library and Information Services
University of Maryland, College Park, Maryland 20742

Printed in the United States of America

CONTENTS

SUBJECT RETRIEVAL IN THE SEVENTIES

OPENING ADDRESS

Dr. James W. Liesener, *Acting Dean*
School of Library and Information Services

The faculty of the School of Library and Information Services here at Maryland has been interested in the area of classification and the organization of knowledge from the beginning of the school in 1965. We have also been very lucky in being able to attract a continuing series of outstanding visiting faculty members from a number of different countries.

In conjunction with this emphasis in the school and this representation on our faculty, in the past few years we have conducted a number of conferences and institutes focusing on developments in the area of classification and the organization of knowledge. Some of you may have attended some of those or be aware of them through reading the proceedings. This present symposium is the second international symposium conducted in the area by the School; the first being held in 1966.

Again, this time, we feel very fortunate that we were able to attract such an outstanding group of speakers with international reputations and internationally representative, and also, we feel very pleased and encouraged at this time of restricted travel funds that we have had so much interest expressed in this conference and that we have a very broad range of institutions, agencies and areas represented.

On behalf of the University, and on behalf of the faculty and staff of the School of Library and Information Services I would like to welcome you to this Symposium: I hope that you will find the next two days rewarding and interesting and I hope that you will feel free to call on any of us for any assistance which you may need.

1

SUBJECT RETRIEVAL IN THE SEVENTIES — METHODS, PROBLEMS, PROSPECTS

HANS (HANAN) WELLISCH
School of Library and Information Services
University of Maryland

The subject approach to books in national, academic and public libraries is difficult and no more than about 30% of all subject searches in catalogs are successful. The present system of subject retrieval by means of Library of Congress (L.C.) *Subject Headings* is critically examined and found to be not effective because there are no firm principles to guide their formation or application. However, the system is believed to be highly reliable because it is linked to the bibliographical description of books which is indeed highly accurate. Librarians are generally able to use L.C. subject headings because they know their pitfalls, but library users find them frustrating. The MARC project simply mechanizes the existing system but does not improve it conceptually.

The formation of subject headings should follow strict rules, derived from General Systems theory and the principles of subject analysis developed during the last 30 years. L.C. *Subject headings* should be augmented by terms taken from specialized thesauri, when terms on a certain level of specificity could be linked to those at other levels (and in other thesauri) by means of common classification codes (possibly UDC). Only the principal subject headings for a book would be displayed on cards, more specific ones being stored in a computer for future retrieval purposes (similar to MEDLARS procedure). Subject headings should be applied so as to generate a co-extensive string of descriptors (as in the PRECIS system), leaving the degree of specificity of indexing terms to individual libraries. The L.C. *Subject Catalog* would then truly serve as a national subject catalog and would make individual subject cataloging largely redundant. Subject catalogs must be geared to the real needs of the user. These needs should be studied in order to create systems that respond to human beings as library users, not those of imaginary "scholars".

The title of this symposium implies some questions: Should subject retrieval in the seventies be different from what went on in previous decades? Is there anything basically wrong with subject retrieval as we know it? Are the users of information in the seventies a breed different from those which librarians have served in the past? If so, are there really new directions? And is there a new panacea for the ills that beset our systems for provision of information?

2

The speakers you will hear today and tomorrow think that the answer to most of these questions is in the affirmative, although, I believe, none of them would think that there is a panacea, as there are no such things in general and therefore librarianship, too, has to manage without a magic wand that would transform everything into the best of all possible worlds. The most we can hope for is to be able to change in this rapidly changing world so as not to be left behind as musty relics from bygone days.

Traditional subject retrieval methods

Libraries — and I include under this term every formal document storage and retrieval system, even if some of them now prefer to call themselves information centers — have one central objective and raison d'être: "That there is a certain piece of . . . information* which is to be timely brought to its potential user in the most effective way and in a suitable and sufficiently complete form."(1)

Our present document retrieval methods normally allow us to find a "piece of information" either by author, by title or by subject. Here, we shall concern ourselves with the latter aspect only, especially since the retrieval methods for the author and title approach are very well developed and few if any complaints have lately been heard about their effectiveness. (This does not necessarily mean that users of catalogs are always able to find documents by author or by title, but failure to do so is the result of faulty memory or sketchy references rather than technical shortcomings of librarians and catalogers, as has been found out in recent experiments.) (2,3,4)

More specifically, we shall look mainly at the problems of subject retrieval in large national, academic and public libraries. There is now indeed a sharp dichotomy between these libraries and special libraries serving particular needs and a well-defined group of users in a special subject field. Special libraries were established mainly during the last 25 years in the U.S., in Europe and elsewhere and it was felt very early that traditional methods of subject retrieval were inadequate for the highly specific topics dealt with in modern documents and for the needs of their sophisticated users. They turned to other methods and experimented with different approaches. It is true that in doing so, the wheel was reinvented over and over again and some of the newly-invented wheels were not even quite round or well-oiled, but after much trial and error, frustrations and achievements, certain insights were gained and principles were discovered that pointed the way to better methods and a deeper understanding of subject retrieval from document collections.

---

*The orginal formulation is "piece of *scientific* information", but the authors' definition of "scientific" is so broad that practically all written information (not only the results of scientific investigation in the conventional sense) is included.

National, academic and large public libraries, however, continue to
this very day to serve their public by subject catalogs constructed
according to principles and methods that date back almost a century
and in some cases even longer. It is true that not too many complaints
against the subject catalog have been voiced by the users of libraries
(although from time to time librarians have done so, apparently without
much success). Yet the phenomenon that a large portion of what used
to be called "scholarly readers" and which we now call researchers,
scientists and engineers is increasingly served by special libraries and their
more sophisticated methods is not only due to the shift of interest from
books to periodicals, reports and semi-published material, but also to the
fact that the subject content of books and periodicals is often virtually
inaccessible in academic libraries, where it is carefully hidden behind
inadequate or antiquated subject headings.

Some of the catalog studies mentioned before make it seem as if the
subject approach to documents were not very widespread among library
users and that most of them look for authors and titles and turn to subject enquiries only when other attempts to locate books fail. But such
results tend rather to emphasize the fact that subject retrieval in present
day dictionary catalogs is both difficult and frustrating, so that the
users of libraries *nolens volens* have to try other avenues of approach
to achieve their aim—to find documents on a certain subject. Students in
universities are now largely provided with ready-made reading lists compiled by their professors and are rarely encouraged to do their own search
in a certain subject field. (This is true for graduate students no less than
for undergraduates.) No wonder, then, that author searches dominate
in university libraries, since authors' names rather than subjects are what
students are systematically taught to look for. The large number of title
searches is probably also due to the same "reading-list syndrome", but
there is also an additional factor discernable in several of the above mentioned studies: titles are almost never cited exactly, but the large majority
of title-based searches produces variations of the original title, where
synonyms and permutations of terms make up the largest part of those
titles that were recognizable at all.(5) In other words, users are in reality
groping for subject terms and convert these to form part of an imaginary title. As to the ability of subject catalogs to satisfy genuine subject searches, one of the most thorough studies comes to the conclusion
that "about 75% of the query terms used by the searchers who did subject searches matched a catalog entry, either exactly or partially".(6)
This seems to be not too bad, but when we look at what is accepted
as "partial match" the picture becomes less encouraging: a quest for
"social pathology" is considered to be adequately matched by the heading "social medicine", because the first word of the term happened to

match exactly; another search for "French theater" is considered to have found a partial match in the heading "French literature—20 century-History and criticism" again on the strength of the first word matching. Now this is stretching the concept of a match (even a partial one) a bit far and I believe most people would rather consider it a mismatch: French theater is a subject covering not only the 20th century and need not be related to either history or criticism, but even if the question turned out to have been on 20th century French theater, then a search in the file labeled "French literature—20 century-History and criticism" would mean that probably hundreds of entries would have to be looked up, of which only a few would actually have been on French theater. And a third example taken from the same paper declares a search for "Election laws" partially matched by the heading "Elections—U.S.—Statistics". Again, the first word matches, but whether Laws are equivalent to Statistics I leave for you to decide. If such "partial matching" is considered to be a successful solution to subject queries, then probably the authors when buying a plane ticket to San Francisco would be satisfied with one to San Antonio, Texas. The figure 75% matches between query terms and subject headings observed in this study must therefore be considerably adjusted: the combined data for tests made in a general library, an undergraduate library, a medical library and a public library show that there were almost 60% exact matches; if we add to these a generously estimated 5% successful partial matches of the morphemic type (variants in spellings, plural versus singular form, etc.) but exclude "partial matches" of the type considered above, the net result is, that present-day cataloging practices satisfy about 65% of all subject term searches. This still does not sound bad, maybe, unless we turn the figures around to say that 35% or *more than a third* of all searches for subject terms are *not* satisfied by current subject indexing practices! Now one must add to all this the fact (also revealed by the same study) that more than half of the searchers who failed in their first attempt to locate a book gave up the search. Although it is stated that the reasons for this behavior are not known and should be further studied, one such reason might be tentatively suggested. Users of libraries have been told that subject catalogs are marvellous and almost infallible tools constructed along lines laid down by the Library of Congress; they are therefore under the impression that if a first search does not lead to results, then one could as well give up: if it's not in the catalog, then it doesn't exist in this library. Be that as it may, however, the stark fact remains that this high "drop-out rate" adds to the already large number of failures when a subject search is performed, so that possibly fewer than 30% of all subject searches are successful. We can only conclude that those retrieval tools which are proudly called subject catalogs somehow do not perform effectively.

The effectiveness of subject catalogs

Clearly something is wrong with the methods used in conventional subject retrieval systems. So let us look now at the methods presently employed and how they affect the effectiveness of our catalogs. For the purpose of the present discussion, we have limited ourselves to national, academic and public libraries which still serve the over-whelming majority of library users. Practically all of them use either the Library of Congress (LC) or Dewey Decimal (DC) classification system to indicate the principal subject matter of a document (or at least that subject which seems to be the most important one to the cataloger, a view that might or might not coincide with that of prospective users). Essentially, this defines only the place of a document on the shelves and makes it possible to find it as a physical entity. Few librarians would today subscribe to the view that these are also good systems for the display of the subject content of books, since unfortunately books and other documents nowadays no longer deal with one single subject but with two, three, or more topics and their inter-relationship which somehow do not lend themselves to compression into a single notation, be it LC or DC. This being so, almost all libraries in this country have always employed a system of alphabetical subject indexing relying on the Library of Congress' *Subject Headings*.(7) (Since Sears' *List of subject headings* is essentially an abridgment of the LC work with only slight modifications, one may say that also the smaller public libraries, which use the Sears' list, rely on LC.) Any discussion, therefore, of the system of subject retrieval used by the majority of libraries in this country must necessarily be a discussion of the subject indexing system used by the Library of Congress. There is no other.

Now, effectiveness of a system is generally defined as the extent to which the goals of a system are achieved. But this definition is an over-simplification, because any system, and particularly one that sets out to perform a service, must be evaluated from several points of view: one is the effectiveness as viewed by the operators of the system, another one is effectiveness as seen by the users. These two views do not necessarily coincide but a system can be considered to be truly effective only if they do. I submit that as far as subject retrieval in our libraries is concerned, there is indeed a wide gap, not to say a chasm between the two, although for a peculiar reason the vast dimensions of this gap are not always recognized.

In order to understand the nature and quality of the system we deal with, we must look at the product that it is designed to deliver: a document surrogate (in the form of a catalog card or a bibliographical entry in a book catalog) on which two different kinds of information are given: one is the physical description of the document, including an indication of its authorship if such can be found or, in some cases, tortuously construed, the other one is an indication of the topics dealt with in the document or, in Fairthorne's words, its "aboutness".(8) Although we are here concerned with the latter aspect, it is necessary to digress for a few moments and look at the characteristics of the former one because here is one of the important clues to an erroneous evaluation of the system and its effectiveness.

For more than 130 years catalogers have spent an enormous amount of time and energy on the most exact and minute bibliographical description of documents. Codes of rules have been devised and revised to cover every conceivable physical aspect of a document, every possible kind of authorship and form of an author's name, and every diacritical mark in the transliteration of non-Roman alphabets. It would be difficult, if not impossible, to improve on the exactness with which each and every document is described and the standards by which this part of cataloging is done by the Library of Congress have justly been acknowledged as the highest possible ones against which all other cataloging is measured. Now, one of the peculiar characteristics of a bibliographical system is the fact that its operators are at the same time also its users, and, even though they constitute only a tiny fraction of the whole user population, they operate the system to some degree for their own good. In this respect, the bibliographical retrieval system is unlike other systems whether in production or in service: the manufacturer of soap does not necessarily have to use his own product to keep clean, and a doctor working in a public health service need not rely on that same service if he himself is ill. But the cataloger, painstakingly noting down even the most minute detail of a document does so primarily not out of concern for the large mass of readers in libraries most of whom could not care less whether the date of publication has been printed on the recto or the verso of the title page, or what is the exact number of roman-numbered pages, unnumbered leaves or height in centimeters (a unit of measurement, by the way, which is a mystery to 99% of the American people). He does so for himself and for his fellow catalogers around the country, in other words: descriptive cataloging is performed at the highest possible level because of the needs of specialists (and on the assumption that the non-specialists, i.e. the large mass of users, can always ignore those data not needed). The general public, through decades of exposure to the product of the Library of Congress and other academic libraries following its example and trying to conform as much as possible to its rules, has become conditioned to see a catalog entry as a highly sophisticated product whose reliability of data is almost 100% (as indeed it is in most cases), although parts of it are neither useful nor intelligible to the non-librarian.(9)

Here, then, we have a situation where input effectiveness is high, while the output is truly effective for only a small minority of users (professional librarians and bibliographers) but is largely wasted on the majority of users.

Let us now return to the subject indexing aspect. As we all know, the subject headings for a document appear on the document surrogate as tracings and in a well-kept catalog there will be multiple entries, each one displaying a different subject heading in its proper place. Since these subject headings are an integral part of the product which both librarians and the public at large have come to regard as a paragon of quality, in the minds of most users it has become an axiom that the LC subject headings are necessarily of the same high standard as the bibliographical data and that the same painstaking care has been extended both in their formation and in their use for the indication of the "aboutness" of documents. This, I submit, is a grand and dangerous delusion.

The shortcomings of present subject headings

Let us first look at the formation of subject headings or the organization of the access vocabulary as represented by LC *Subject headings*. The weighty volume of 1432 pages with its many thousands of headings and cross-references has not only forbidding dimensions but is also an almost impenetrable maze in which most seekers soon get lost. It has been attacked many times in papers, reports and books (10,11,12) and many examples of its inconsistencies, illogicalities and absurdities have been exposed, so that it will be sufficient to cite only a few glaring instances of subject headings apparently designed to retrieve information when in fact they make it well-nigh impossible to find anything at all.

A few months ago, the computer celebrated its 25th birthday and the literature about it has been with us for about the same length of time. But the term "Computer" is still not a recognized term in the Library of Congress and therefore in all libraries that follow its practice and therefore in practically all places in which people presumably look for literature on the computer. Some unknown genius decided 25 years ago that "Computer" was not an acceptable "name" in Cutter's sense and so he set about to invent the phrase ELECTRONIC CALCULATING MACHINE (which is about the equivalent of some Iroquois Indian tribes calling a horse "one rides on its back"). We have been stuck with it ever since. It means that whoever has the peculiar idea to look for material on computers under the word "Computer" will at best find a "see" reference leading him to ELECTRONIC CALCULATING MACHINES, and at worst he will not even find that. But this is not the whole story. When the computer came of age and different kinds of "electronic calculating machines" were invented, such as Analog computers and Digital computers, they were listed by LC as ELECTRONIC ANALOG COMPUTERS and ELECTRONIC DIGITAL COMPUTERS and not, as one might have expected under "Digital electronic calculating machines" or even as "Electronic calculating machines, digital" (which would at least have brought together all material on various kinds of computers under one heading, however awkward). Still later, Hybrid computers were invented (combining certain features of both analog and digital computers) and they were listed by LC as HYBRID COMPUTERS, dropping in this case the epithet ELECTRONIC without any explanation. Then, computers began to perform all sorts of non-numerical tasks, such as COMPUTER GRAPHICS, so entered by LC and not, as you might have come to expect, as "Electronic calculating machine graphics", and we have also COMPUTER MUSIC, but when you look for "Computer circuits", back you go to square one to look under ELECTRONIC CALCULATING MACHINES — CIRCUITS. "Computer programming" is another matter again: it has been entered as PROGRAMMING (ELECTRONIC COMPUTERS), where all of a sudden the by now well-known "Electronic calculating machines" have become "Electronic computers". And so it goes. These are by no means all possible combinations, permutations and configurations of different terms for the same concept, but enough has been said to show that neither is it possible to find material on the subject "Computers" and its sub-divisions in one alphabetical place, nor can anyone guess in which places and under which names these concepts have been indexed.

One might think that "Libraries", having been with us for more than 3000 years would fare better than such new-fangled things as computers, so that terminology would be more uniform. But as most of you know, we have in the LC list LIBRARIES as well as LIBRARIES, CHILDREN'S versus SCHOOL LIBRARIES; LIBRARIES, NAVAL versus MILITARY LIBRARIES; LIBRARIES, CATHOLIC versus JEWISH LIBRARIES and LIBRARIES, SPECIAL versus MUSIC LIBRARIES. Quite recently, not more than three years ago, the Library of Congress discovered that there are also Public Libraries whereupon these space-age institutions were immediately so entered (although you will not find them in the current edition of LC *Subject headings*). The chances, then, of finding documents on any kind of library either under the term LIBRARIES or under a specific designation are about fifty-fifty and whether you score a hit or a miss when turning to the catalog is an even bet. If you want to find material on libraries for black people, however, all bets are off, because you find it only under the phrase LIBRARIES AND NEGROES, after you have exhausted all direct and indirect headings beginning with LIBRARIES . . .

Another source of frustration is the ad hoc invention of "phrase headings" for subjects that do not conform to any of the existing headings or are otherwise not "nameable" in Cutter's sense. I shall give you just one example. The book by H. R. Hahn *Helping the retarded to know God* (LC 73-99315) is indexed under RELIGIOUS EDUCATION OF

THE MENTALLY HANDICAPPED. Now, such a sentence would possibly make a good telegraphic abstract, but as a subject heading, it serves only to bury the book forever. Anyone interested in the subject would probably look under MENTALLY HANDICAPPED which is a valid LC heading, but the cataloger decided not to put it there. Only if one happens to think about the word RELIGIOUS could he find it, although he would, of course, have to wade through hundreds of other entries beginning with this word, and even under RELIGIOUS EDU-CATION there would be a large number of books not at all concerned with the mentally handicapped.

Subject indexing: "general" vs. "specific"

So much for the quality of the vocabulary itself. Turning now to the application of these subject headings to documents, we have been told many times that there is an almost irreconcilable dilemma between in-dexing for the "general" reader and indexing for the "specialist". Sey-mour Lubetzky says that "Users of the large catalog differ greatly and require at least two basic types of subject records. The non-research user requires a selective subject catalog . . . the scholar and research user of the catalog . . . requires a comprehensive subject record. His subject needs may be said to include the following questions: 1. What sources of information exist on a given subject? 2. Which of the sources are available in the given library? 3. Where are the other sources avail-able?"(13) Although it is true that there are important differences in the way in which "non-research" users and "scholars" ask for documents, it does not seem to follow that the three search objectives are not equally valid for both types of user. Where one is selective and the other compre-hensive is not so much in the choice of a subject heading for a document but in the *use* made of one or more documents found in the subject catalog under this heading. On the same subject, Patricia B. Knapp states that "Catalog users . . . range from the person who wants a single reference on a subject to the one who wants to assemble all the library holdings in a given field, large or small . . . At present the subject catalog attempts to serve in some measure both types of use."(14) As we shall presently see, the subject catalog fails many times in this attempt not because "some measure" cannot be found to serve the needs of both types of users (and presumably the needs of some users who fall in between these two extremes) but because subject headings are applied by LC with neither objective in mind.

There is, first of all, a tendency to bury bothersome details or aspects of subjects, especially if they defy "naming" in Cutter's sense, under some more general but "nameable" heading, with the result that some-times an unbelievable number of documents are listed together under one single heading. This serves neither generalist nor specialist, since few people have enough patience to flip through some 2000 cards, all labeled "Child psychology" to find a book on "The ape and the child". This technique sometimes also results in entirely misleading subject headings, especially when the "unnamed" subject of the book is aggravated by the fact that it is written in a foreign language. Thus, for example, the book by André Lheritier *Les physiologies 1840-1845; bibliographie descriptive* (LC no. 68-130269) is indexed only under BIBLIOGRAPH- IES (i.e. the techniques of bibliographical work) whereas it is in fact a descriptive catalog of a collection of physiological treatises in the Bibliothèque nationale. A Swedish book by Ove Hahn, *Jazz, kyrka, och ungdom* (Jazz, church, and youth) (LC no. 57-23880) can be found only under JAZZ MUSIC, where as the aspects that make this book unique and different from hundreds of general books on jazz, namely the influence of this music on religious life and on young people in Sweden, are totally neglected.

But even when it is somehow recognized that a general subject should be further specified by the application of subheadings, the practice does not seem to follow any discernible pattern, as shown by Jessica L. Harris; "The so-called aspect subdivisions which are actually accidents of termi- nology are applied regardless of the number of titles entered under the heading . . . It was not possible to find firm evidence of application (or non-application) of true subdivisions (i.e. . . . treatment of the entire subject from a special point of view) in this manner"(15)

And as Harry Dewey has shown (16) a book on *Ornamental Dis- play of Dahlias for the Novice* may first be indexed under DAHLIAS and FLOWER ARRANGING, later maybe under DAHLIAS-AR- RANGING, and much later with the added subheading DAHLIAS- ARRANGING-POPULAR WORKS, depending not on a value judge- ment on whether the heading will best serve the interests of the generalist or the specialist, but based purely and simply on the sheer *number* of books that accumulated in the Library of Congress under the main part of the heading! Even though a case could conceivably be made for such a practice as far as the Library of Congress itself is concerned, it becomes disastrous when adopted blindly by hundreds of libraries all over the country and also abroad, irrespective of whether they have the same kind and number of books on the subject and whether they serve the general public or the specialist.

If we now contrast this picture with the treatment of descriptive data in a catalog, we find that the difference in quality is indeed appalling. Certainly, no cataloger with a minimum of self-respect would tolerate descriptive cataloging data such as the spelling of authors' names, the recording of titles and editions, not to speak of numbers of pages (roman, arabic or otherwise) that were incorrect, wrong or plain non-existant in one out of every two entries. The mind boggles to imagine the hue and cry that would ensue if such shoddy cataloging practices were allowed in national, academic and public libraries. Yet in the field of subject indexing it is exactly such shoddiness, incompleteness and general inadequacy that is not only tolerated but thought to be an acceptable norm.

Our subject catalogs—ineffective tools

Our large libraries, then, construct and maintain at great cost catalogs which are almost 100% effective in the bibliographic description of physical entities and very good at the identification of persons or corporate bodies responsible for the creation and contents of documents— but fall down on their job of making these documents accessible for those who look for ideas and subjects, and either do not know or do not care who wrote a particular book or what its exact title is.

Not many users of libraries have gone on record to tell us what they think about the effectiveness and reliability of a subject retrieval system which does not deserve the name of a system at all but is a hotchpotch of guesswork, prejudice, and preconception. Faced with the necessity to use it and having been told that it conforms to the highest possible standards, they reluctantly conclude that this is apparently how far one can go in subject retrieval when using libraries. Whereupon they try anything to avoid such places like the plague and turn to them only in dire need or in inclement weather, after all other avenues of information gathering have proved to be inaccessible or have produced negative results. This much we know now from innumerable user needs studies among scientists and engineers as well as among those most elusive characters, the "general readers".

Yet the defenders of the system in the library world have repeatedly tried to tell us that it is "a marvellous tool and very productive once you get by the language problem".(17) Such a statement, however self-seeking and foolish it may be, is proof for the differences that prevail in evaluating the effectiveness of the system. The operators of the system have no grounds to doubt its effectiveness: it has been adopted by thousands of libraries (a fact that, incidentally, surprised the operators quite some as far back as 1916 when the Librarian of Congress stated that "there was . . . no expectation that the scheme would be adopted by other libraries; much less was there any profession that it would be suited to their needs . . . Under the circumstances, the number of libraries that are already adopting it in whole or in part is somewhat surprising."(18) and the sales of L. C. catalogue cards reached the unprecedented figure of more than 80 million cards in 1970, the larger part of which were sets of multiple cards used for subject entries.

From the user's point of view, we must again differentiate sharply between the operators as users, in other words, trained librarians, and the millions of non-librarians who expect guidance from the system in their subject searches. Librarian-users presumably find the system quite effective, if we are to judge from statements like Shell's, quoted above. The operative part must be seen in the qualification "once you get by the language problem". Naturally, the subject cataloger or reference librarian who has used the big red book for years, has assigned subject headings from it and is familiar with its pitfalls, has no "language problem". If approached at the reference desk for material on Computers, his mind will almost automatically flip to "Electronic calculating machines" and he will presumably also remember to look under "Libraries, Children's" when asked for material on Children's Libraries while immediately reaching for drawer S when asked for "School libraries". Occasionally, even he will encounter difficulties, such as when a book on the history of drug use is indexed under "MEDICINE, MAGIC, MYSTIC, AND SPAGIRIC" but then, you cannot expect 100% efficiency from any system. . .

Not so for the user-at-large. No matter how proficient he may be in the English language, he will never be able to outguess the clever cataloger and it would be a remarkable feat indeed if he would be able to find what a library has on Computers or Libraries or on almost anything by following up all headings, cross-references and different combinations. When testing the attempt of users to find subjects with the aid of LC subject headings, Dorothy A. Day found that "Classification of a subject [heading] as 'usable' sometimes assumes unlimited patience on the part of the patron in dealing with the catalog, for it includes anything which can be traced, directly or through cross references, to the actual subject heading used, and sometimes ploughing through all cards under that heading until the exact card is hit upon. This can sometimes involve upwards of 600 cards under one heading alone, and up to twenty cross references to be checked."(19)

We must conclude, then, that the effectiveness of the system used for subject retrieval in the overwhelming majority of libraries leaves much to be desired and shows, in fact, the characteristics of all monopolistic systems: it satisfies the needs of its operators but does not care too much about the needs of its users, in providing them with over-elaborate descriptive data for which there is little or no demand, while shortchanging them with woefully inadequate and sometimes outright misleading subject retrieval tools.

The managers' viewpoint

There is, however, a third factor interested in the performance of any system and we have not said anything about it so far. The *managers* or *fund allocators* look at the system first of all from the point of view of efficiency—they want to make sure that the system works at the least cost to the greatest possible satisfaction. In other words, they want value for their money. Up to now, most managers have been satisfied to hear that so and so many hundreds of thousands of books have been "handled" annually by a library and they did not care too much about what kind of "handling" was involved. But I think that we are rapidly approaching the point in time when managers and legislators will understand that information is not a commodity to be counted by the piece like so many heads of cattle, boxes of cereal or cars rolling off the assembly line. When complaints about libraries become louder and more numerous, when the tremendous proliferation of catalog cards or ever larger volumes of book catalogs produced by computer printout does little more than add weight to the already overloaded floors of libraries, when it will be realized that literally billions of dollars are spent on the technical perfection of a product that satisfies the needs of only a few, while the legitimate needs of millions of users who seek information are sorely neglected because they are handled by a system that was conceived one hundred years ago and has not been changed appreciably ever since—then, I am afraid, the operators of the system will be in for an unpleasant surprise.

Subject retrieval and MARC

There are many library administrators and catalogers, however, who think that they have nothing to fear and that, in fact, the cataloging millenium is near, because we now have the MARC tapes. Given enough programmers, machine time and money, all problems of bibliographical control and subject retrieval will be solved by the computer, and everything will be just hunky-dory. Now, the MARC project is truly a remarkable achievement and I am sure that it will revolutionize the world of bibliography, as it might indeed lead to the fulfillment of Konrad Gesner's dream of the *Bibliotheca universalis* in our own time. The whole library world is indebted to the people who were in charge of the design and programming of this project, and who, I presume, often wondered whether they were dealing with librarians and purveyors of knowledge or with a bunch of peculiar pedants who would not relinquish an iota of all the technicalities that had become so dear to them over the decades, and without which apparently no information can be communicated from book to reader. The coding became redundant, the programs became overly complex, the computer printout chains were almost bent out of shape—but finally, the seemingly impossible was achieved: every minute physical detail of every conceivable kind of document can now be transcribed, tagged, stored and retrieved with the utmost accuracy and in any desired combination.

And yet, all those will give us only the outer shell of books. When we want to find out what human minds have thought and what has been preserved between the covers of a book, the MARC tapes still give us the same old LC subject headings with which we have been saddled for decades. That makes MARC rather like a modern jet plane powered by a late nineteenth-century model of a steam engine: the thing might possibly move or even fly, but it will be prone to accidents, unreliable and above all, the streamlined features of the fuselage will be wasted because of the slow speed attained. The MARC tapes carry also LC and DC class numbers, to be sure, but these are no more than mechanical guides to the physical place of a book on the shelves or "marking and parking" devices. As for subject retrieval, both systems suffer from the same faults: they are based on ideas and concepts that had their heyday in the late 19th century, they are not specific enough for modern documents and they are entirely unsuitable for use in mechanized retrieval systems. All attempts made so far to show that either LC or DC can be "mechanized" are either motivated by a pious wish to show at all costs that antiquated systems can be "modernized", or they suffer from sheer ignorance about the basic requirements of mechanized subject retrieval. This does not necessarily mean that LC or DC class marks cannot be used as shelf marks. If a roughly grouped linear display of volumes is considered to be useful in a library, then these systems will function more or less well and there is really very little difference between them as to their effectiveness on open shelves. But we should not delude ourselves or our readers to believe that MARC tapes carrying LC or DC class numbers or LC subject headings are reliable subject retrieval devices. Computerized means of frustration and electronically encoded ineptitude are no better than the manually produced variety. Indeed, they are more dangerous: the very fact that these haphazardly chosen, illogical and prejudiced subject headings have been put on a most sophisticated and modern communication vehicle and that they can be handled by machines has already made them still more respectable, not to say venerable, than they were before. Library administrators around the country are now convinced that by adopting the MARC tapes they have automatically also acquired the very latest and best in retrieval capabilities, not realizing that the mere computerization of traditional forms and tools has not made them any more modern or useful. The medium is not the message, whatever you may have been told. The message is still what human beings have said about events, things, and emotions and how they preserved it for the benefit of other human beings in documents. And this message still awaits an effective retrieval tool, geared to human beings in the latter part of the 20th century, to their environment, their needs and their aspirations.

The MARC tapes have a tremendous potential as such a subject retrieval tool of the highest quality if — and that is a big if — the subject analysis is performed not only centrally but also by entirely different methods and at a different level. If this could be achieved, there would really be little need for libraries of any kind, including even special libraries, to do their own subject indexing: the centrally provided headings would index the subjects of books exhaustively, while at the same time provision would be made for different degrees of specificity.

Some possible remedies

What can be done to achieve this aim? I am afraid that after all the harsh words I have said about the Library of Congress and its subject headings, those of you who are using the system and especially those in this audience who are actually engaged in its formation and development will look forward to the climax: Ecrasez l'infâme! Not so, my friends. We have to be realists and pragmatists, as indeed the profession of librarianship is essentially a pragmatic business, by whatever name you call it: to serve as a link between people who had something to say and wrote it down and people who are eager to learn what others have said. We cannot close our eyes to the fact that practically all national, academic and public libraries in this country and many such libraries abroad are geared to this system and are neither willing nor able to throw it out the window. But then, neither are the LC *Subject headings* the Law given on Mount Sinai. They can be changed, they can be augmented, and, above all, their use and application can be made more effective and meaningful. Let us consider each of these points in turn.

Change in the structure of subject headings

Changes should be made in the structure of the subject heading system, starting from basic principles and applying the findings of General Systems Theory as well as modern methods of subject analysis, both of which were developed during the last 30 years, giving us a much better insight into the nature and problems of subject retrieval. The results should be a set of firm rules for the construction of subject headings and the establishment of a coherent network of cross references between them—not, as today, based on unfounded assumptions on what readers "prefer" or are "apt to think about", but on clear and consistent principles. It goes without saying that once the system has been based on such general principles, it will become easier to use and will lead to better consistency than the present jumble, because subject indexers will be able to make their decisions relying on a logical and coherent framework of terms. By the same token, it will be possible to instruct readers about the effective use of subject catalogs and subject indexes where at present one cannot even attempt to do so because of the chaotic nature of subject headings.

Augmentation of subject headings

Augmentation of the system can be performed at several levels and might take several forms. First of all, the basic list of terms can and should be more specific than it is now, especially in the fields of science and technology. It is now easier to do this than it might have been even ten years ago, since we have thesauri covering the major disciplines of engineering, chemistry, biology, agriculture, medicine and others. Although admittedly none of these is perfect in its choice and arrangement of terms, they constitute a reasonably good consensus of what current terminology in these fields is and will certainly do much to eliminate outmoded or artificially contrived subject terms presently used by LC. The incorporation of a kind of thesaurus terms is, incidentally, already an accepted practice in LC *Subject headings,* although few people are aware of this. I am referring to the practice of adding the LC class number and its verbal equivalent to some subject headings (although the terms taken from the classification scheme cannot themselves be used as subject headings). In many instances, the classification terms are clearer or more specific than the term in *Subject headings* and it would not be a bad idea to allow their use as additional headings. The addition of the relevant LC number forms the link between the two complementary systems. This is exactly what has recently been proposed as a general method for "reconciling" thesauri in the same subject field using different terminology or thesauri in different but related subject fields that have to be made compatible in order to allow for mutual use of documents indexed by them.(20) We might ultimately arrive at a list of subject headings in which each permitted term is coded by a numerical system that in turn leads to a term or group of terms in any of the more specialized thesauri from which libraries serving specialists could take further, more precise terms for more specific indexing. Let me give you an example to show what could be done in this way.

The book by A. M. Yassin, *Mean roughness coefficient in open channels with different roughnesses of bed and side walls* is meticulously cataloged as far as bibliographical details are concerned (fig. 1) but its

Yassin, Ahmed Mostafa, 1923-

Mean roughness coefficient in open channels with different roughnesses of bed and side walls. Zürich, 1953.

90 p. illus., tables. 23 cm.

Thesis—Eidgenössische Technische Hochschule, Zürich.

Curriculum vitae.

"Erscheint als Mitteilung Nr. 27 der Versuchsanstalt für Wasserbau und Erdbau der Eidgenössischen Technischen Hochschule in Zürich."

Bibliography: p. 90.

1. Hydraulics. I. Title.

TC175.Y34   57-20848

Figure 1.

subject is indexed only under HYDRAULICS. This makes the book practically irretrievable because it is buried among hundreds of general textbooks on Hydraulics and specialized treatises on various branches of hydraulics. The "general" reader, if patient enough, will find it at the very end of the file on HYDRAULICS (remember that the author's name begins with the letter Y!) but will not be able to use it because of its specialized treatment of a particular phenomenon, while the specialist interested in Open channel flow and the influence of Roughness on it will not find it under "Flow" or "Flow in open channels" or "Open channels" or "Channels" or "Roughness" because none of these terms exists in the present *Subject Headings.* So the subject heading HYDRAULICS serves neither the general reader nor the specialist. (It would be interesting to know, by the way, whether a subject cataloger in the Library of Congress would place L. Stephen's book *English literature and society in the eighteenth century* under CIVILIZATION— which would be similar to the treatment given to Yassin's book . . .) Assuming now that the LC *Subject headings* were augmented by terms taken from the *Thesaurus of Engineering and Scientific Terms (TEST)* (21) the book would be indexed under FLOW, CHANNEL FLOW, OPEN CHANNEL FLOW and ROUGHNESS while the heading HYDRAULICS could probably be dropped as too general and therefore practically useless. Each of the terms would also be coded by a number that would correspond to the proper subject category in *TEST* where additional terms are listed, to be used in more specialized libraries. The same code numbers would, however, also apply to the still more detailed schedules of terms in the *Water Resources Thesaurus* (22) from which additional terms such as ROUGHNESS COEFFICIENTS, ROUGHNESS (HYDRAULICS), HEAD LOSS and others could be taken by a highly specialized information center indexing Yassin's book. Thus, a fully integrated network of both general and specialized terms, linked and interrelated by code numbers would make the old controversy of "indexing for the general reader versus the specialist" obsolete. Needless to say, computers would have to be used to store vocabularies at different levels of sophistication and for different subject fields, when the linkage via code numbers would be achieved automatically once the semantic network had been established by indexers and subject specialists. Neville (23) suggests the use of arbitrarily chosen code numbers but there is, of course, no reason why an internationally recognized numerical code such as the *Universal Decimal Classification (UDC)* could not serve as such a "switching code", especially since a field for this code has already been reserved on the MARC record. Figure 2 shows how UDC numbers could serve as links between terms now used by *LC Subject headings, TEST* and the *Water Resources Thesaurus.*

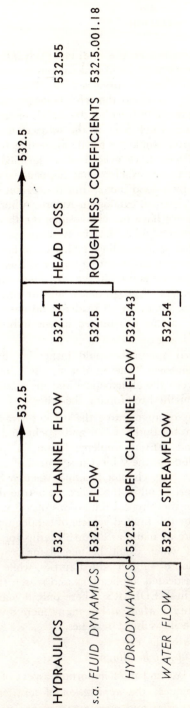

FIGURE 2. USE OF U.D.C. CODES AS LINKS BETWEEN DIFFERENT INDEXING TOOLS

This would introduce the additional advantage of grouping terms in hierarchical order and would make it possible to enter the alphabetically arranged catalog first by using subject headings, then maybe switching to the hierarchy to which the term belongs and scanning it upwards or downwards in order to broaden the search or to narrow it down. At any point, one could switch back to the subject headings where one or more coordinated terms would be listed, suggesting further avenues of search. Those of you who have ever used a classified catalog will, of course, recognize that this is exactly what happens when one scans a classified file supported by a good index. But it does not mean that we should try to impose the classified catalog on American libraries. Again, we have to be realists and we have to acknowledge the fact that ever since Cutter's days the American public has been trained in the use of alphabetical catalogs and this long-standing habit cannot be changed, however useful a classified arrangement might be for subject searches and however much a classified approach is used in the dictionary catalog itself (for example, in the arrangement of geographical and historical headings which make these an eternal puzzle to all readers who have been led to believe that the dictionary catalog is arranged in one unbroken alphabet and is "as easy as ABC").

The proposed approach would rather be similar to the one that is displayed in the new "Thesaurofacet" (24) and it would create a true symbiosis between the alphabetical and the classified approach to subject retrieval, one method reinforcing the other.

Another way of augmenting the present array of subject headings has been proposed by Borko (25) and Richmond (26), following earlier suggestions and partial implementation in project INTREX (27), namely to include in the subject description of a document also keywords taken from the title, chapter headings, section headings, summaries and maybe even part or all of the index. It is true that this could not longer be done within the physical limitations of a 3 x 5 card, but we need not be hampered by this limited vehicle of cataloguing. It would be perfectly possible to store as many as 20 or 30 terms for a book on MARC tape, only 3 or 4 of which would be tagged for printout on cards and automatic generation of subject added entries, while the rest would be stored for more sophisticated applications and search strategies. This is exactly what is done in MEDLARS, where only a maximum of four headings is printed in *Index Medicus* but many more are stored in the computer to assist in specific subject searches.

Co-extensive subject headings

Now to the last and most important aspect of improvement in subject retrieval techniques: the *application* of terms and subject headings to documents. Indexers and users agree on one point: subject headings or index terms should express the topic dealt with in a document, or its "aboutness". Where they disagree is on what exactly constitutes this "aboutness". Different users at different times and places will read a different "aboutness" into the same document, and this in turn is caused by the basic underlying difficulty of defining what "about" means, as shown by various attempts of philosophers and logicians (28, 29). Fairthorne (7) distinguishes between "intensional" and "extensional" aboutness, where the former is related to the question why a document has been acquired or requested, while the latter is concerned with the concepts mentioned in a document, and very aptly draws a parallel between the syntagmatic and paradigmatic dimensions in linguistics. As far as subject indexing for a national collection is concerned, the question of "intensional aboutness" becomes largely irrelevant, because books are acquired by the Library of Congress and by hundreds of academic and research libraries participating in the Farmington plan simply because they exist and happen to find their way to these libraries. As far as users' requests affect "intensional aboutness" the most that can be said is that at any future time a user might ask for just that book—he might be a "general reader" or he might be a specialist and the two might very well be one and the same person.

This leaves us with "extensional aboutness" or the concepts mentioned in a document. In most instances, the use of modern analytical techniques will make it possible to determine what constitutes the main subject or subjects of a book, what are the active and the passive entities, what properties, processes and operations are mentioned and which relationships obtain between them. Such analysis will result in a heading that is "co-extensive" with the book, without having to fall back on "phrase headings" that are the bane of the present system.

Subject indexing and the computer

I have devoted much time to the deficiencies of the principal indexing language used by subject catalogers in this country and the possible ways and means of improving it. But it would be foolish to overlook the fact that many of the shortcomings in subject retrieval are caused by ignorance and inconsistency on the part of human indexers. With the advent of the computer, many people (especially if they were not too familiar with the art of indexing) thought that machines could be taught to index well and consistently, thereby eliminating the need for costly and unreliable human indexers. Much research has gone into attempts to solve this problem, but its satisfactory and economical solution is not yet in sight and the prospects for computerized subject indexing are, at least for the seventies, rather dim. This is so because (a) our present knowledge of linguistics is insufficient to instruct computers in the art of indexing; (b) all attempts at automatic indexing rely on the availability of the full text of documents in machine-readable form, a condition that will not be fulfilled in the foreseeable future for even a fraction of the documents collected by libraries; and (c) the costs of even limited experiments in automatic indexing show that this is a prohibitively costly business (and one that probably will not become cheaper with full-scale production).

But we should not only try to find the answer to the question 'Can computers do indexing?" To my mind, we should rather be concerned about the question "*Should* computers index books?" If books were written by computers for computers, it is certain that they could also be indexed by computers, because the books would necessarily have been written by an algorithm, and once you have an algorithm for a set of symbols, it is relatively easy to devise an algorithm for any sub-set of these symbols. But documents are written by human beings for other human beings and it seems to me that this is the principal reason why they should also be indexed by human beings—not because human indexers are necessarily always better than machines in doing this, but because they are able to detect meanings, shades of meanings and subtle significances that cannot possibly be reduced to algorithms because our present knowledge of perception, cognition and linguistics is simply not sufficient to do this. And as long as we do not know how human beings go about performing indexing tasks we cannot even hope to be able to teach this art to machines. The conclusions reached about machine translation (which is now pretty much considered to be unattainable) apply also to indexing which, after all, is nothing but a special case of translating—casting the language of a document into the mold of another, more compressed and concentrated languge.

Computer-*aided* indexing, however, is quite another matter. Once a co-extensive heading has been constructed for a book by following a prescribed routine of subject analysis, a computer can be harnessed to the task of generating rotated headings and displaying every major term in its full context, as has been demonstrated by the application of the PRECIS system to the British National Bibliography (BNB) (30).

There is no reason to assume that the Library of Congress cannot do what is now being done by BNB. When assigning an original subject heading, it should be as *extensive* as possible in its indexing, covering all principal concepts dealt with in a book as expressed in its title, chapter headings, foreword or abstract and using a structured vocabulary that is kept current and at a level of specificity comparable to that of thesauri in general disciplines. The degree of specificity of indexing would then become a matter for the individual library to consider, when more specific terms might be added as needed from specialized thesauri and lists, aided by the network of codes and corresponding terms outlined above.

Re-allocation of priorities in cataloging

It is true that such a degree of analysis would take more time than is spent on subject heading work at present. But when we consider that LC subject indexing which was originally done for this great library alone and which was only gradually accepted also by other libraries with different needs, is now practically performed for the whole country and soon also for other countries, then we cannot escape the conclusion that LC, once having shouldered this responsibility, must assume it to a much larger extent than has been the case hitherto. If the means at its disposal do not allow for more than a certain maximum time being spent on any one book, then it has to be re-examined to which tasks this time is to be allocated. It has not been unknown in the past that a cataloger had to hunt up the dates of birth and death of an obscure author for days on end, spending untold hours on just that detail. Although I am convinced that this is now no longer the case, I still have a feeling that much more care and time are devoted to descriptive cataloging than to the subject analysis of books and that the latter is sometimes done by a fleeting glance at the title page, clutching at seemingly significant words in the title and then classifying and indexing the book in a matter of minutes, without giving much thought to its subject content. If you think that this happens only in fields with which the subject cataloguers are not very familiar (especially in science and technology), look at the books that have been classified and indexed during the last five years in class Z 1001 General bibliography. You will find there a peculiar mixture of heterogeneous subjects and corresponding unsuitable subject headings—and remember that the subject is Librarianship, a field in which every cataloger should be a specialist!

But not only re-allocation of resources and re-assessment of priorities are urgently needed. The whole library profession must put its weight behind a constant drive for substantially increased allocations to the central source of subject retrieval tools. The Library of Congress, far from being able to "absorb" cuts in its budget (absorption meaning curtailment of services to its users), must receive massive support in order to enable it to transform its retrieval tools into the unparalleled national assets they could be. As Lubetzky wrote: ". . . the Library of Congress *Subject Catalog* already provides an instrument which could be readily and effectively employed [for the production of a national subject record]. When this comes to pass, as eventually it must, the Library of Congress *Subject Catalog* will become a national subject record and all the libraries represented in it will be able to dispense with their own subject catalogs, except for local current selective lists. The national subject catalog, as a current bibliographical record, will contribute far more to the scholar's question of what sources of information exist on his subject of interest . . . It will, of course, also facilitate the adoption of new methods and techniques of subject control if and when such are developed." (13)

User feedback

Now, almost twenty years later, the new methods and techniques are here. But their adoption and implementation is, of course, not a matter of money and manpower alone. There must first of all be the genuine will to abandon the outmoded ways of yesterday so that the dead weight of the past will not forever hamper the endeavours to forge better tools for today and tomorrow. To achieve this effectively, we will also need user feedback. Does anyone know how users (and I mean non-librarians) react to our catalogs, whether they are able to use subject headings, whether they know how to make head or tail of headings followed by commas versus headings followed by dashes and other intricacies which have been concocted by librarians over the decades with the proclaimed aim in mind to help the reader? We only know that half of them turn away after the first try and the remaining half does not find what they are looking for, as I pointed out in the beginning. We have not made any sincere efforts to get any feedback from the users of our catalogs and this I see as one of the challenging tasks of the seventies in subject retrieval — finding out what readers really want, what turns them on and what turns them off. In my own country, a modest beginning has been made in this direction: catalogers at the Tel Aviv University Library have to spend a few months every year at the reference desk, using the very same catalog they help to create and coming into contact with users. They get an idea about language and terms currently used by actual readers, they also learn what readers are actually looking for in catalogs and when they return to their desks in the cataloging department they stand a better chance to class and index books in a way that is geared to the real needs of users. I am sure that still other and better ways can be found to feel the pulse of the library's public and to gauge its moods, in order to translate this into search terms that really respond to what people have in mind at a particular time and in a particular place.

Adapting the subject catalog to users' needs

The corollary to such a flexible approach is, of course, a sufficiently flexible indexing medium that is responsive to changes in terminology and in search behaviour without undue financial burdens. In other words: there must be a cheap and reliable technique whereby "electronic calculating machine" can be changed into "computer" without having to handle tens of thousands of records, manually pulling them, erasing the heading on them, writing a new heading on them, and re-filing them in a new place (which is the real reason behind the stubborn existence of those "electronic calculating machines" in LC catalogs).

Also here, the computer can, and I hope will, come to our aid in the seventies: an unsuitable or outmoded heading can be erased from an entry on the MARC tape and a new one can be substituted whereupon new entries can be printed out and properly filed without any difficulty and probably with low cost, if the whole procedure is reasonably well designed. Here again, computer-*aided* catalog maintenance will free us from routines that are today kept up only because "things have always been done that way" and it will transform the subject catalog into a flexible and adaptive tool, responsive to the changing needs of its users.

This will be only one aspect of the inevitable shift from subject retrieval tools as we know them today — rigid, thoroughly mechanistic devices cast into a mold that was devised generations ago — to systems designed with a humanistic outlook. Dr. Wooster some years ago expressed a desire for a "cuddly microreader" (30) because he (and presumably every other human being who ever had to use microforms) was fed up with the bulky and awkward monsters imposed by manufacturers on helpless microform users, and was yearning for something more usable, more flexible, more human. A British librarian, Maurice B. Line, made a plea that information systems should be designed for human beings (32) and not for imaginary robots, and Dr. Rowena Swanson (33) recently argued that "The information business is a people business". This, I hope, is the way subject retrieval will go in the seventies: we must change our systems so they can cope with our rapidly changing world and the growth of recorded knowledge, we must adapt and expand them to cater for the ever-growing needs and the increasing specialization and sophistication of our readers. Above all, we must make them usable — not for an imaginary "scholar" who vanished with the World of Yesterday, nor for an equally phantastic robot-like man who would only push buttons and accept in a docile manner whatever a machine deems fit to present him with — but for human beings in quest of knowledge.

REFERENCES

1. MIKHAILOV, A.I., A.I. CHERNYI and R.S. GILYAREVSKII. "Informatics: Its Scope and Methods." *In: On Theoretical Problems of Informatics.* Moscow, All-Union Institute for Scientific and Technical Information, 1969. (FID 435) p. 14.
2. AYRES, F.H., et al. "Author Versus Title: A Comparative Survey of the Accuracy of the Information Which the User Brings to the Library Catalogue." *Journal of Documentation,* v. 24, no. 4, 1969, p. 266-272.
3. LIPETZ, B.A. *User Requirements in Identifying Desired Works in a Large Library.* New Haven, Yale University Library, 1970.
4. UNIVERSITY OF CHICAGO. Graduate Library School. *Requirements Study for Future Catalogs. Report no. 2 to the National Science Foundation.* Chicago, 1968.
5. ref. (4) p. 20.

6. TAGLIACOZZO, R. and M. KOCHEN. Information-seeking Behavior of Catalog Users. *Information Storage and Retrieval*, v. 6, 1970, p. 363-381.

7. LIBRARY OF CONGRESS. *Subject Headings*. 7th ed. Washington, Govt. Printing Office, 1966.

8. FAIRTHORNE, R.A. "Content Analysis, Specification and Control." *In*: *Annual Review of Information Science and Technology*, v. 4, 1969, p. 73-83.

9. MILLER, R.A. "On the Use of the Card Catalog." *Library Quarterly*, v. 12, 1942, p. 629-637.

10. DAILY, J.E. "Many Changes, No Alterations; an Analysis of Library of Congress *Subject Headings*, Seventh edition. *Library Journal*, v. 92, Nov. 1, 1967, p. 3961-3963.

11. DEWEY, H. "The Relationships between the Headings in the Subject Catalog and the Classification Numbers of the Books. *In*: *Re-classification; rationale and problems. Proc. of a conference* . . . College Park, School of Library and Information Services, University of Maryland, 1968. p. 57-78.

12. COATES, E. *Subject Catalogues: Headings and Structure*. London, Library Association, 1960. Chapter 7.

13. LUBETZKY, S. *Program for Future Development of the Library of Congress General Catalogs*. 1952. (Administrative memorandum) Quoted by J.W. Cronin, *Library Quarterly*, v. 34, no. 1, Jan. 1964, p. 94.

14. KNAPP, P.B. "The Subject Catalog in the College Library." *Library Quarterly*, v. 14, no. 2. 1944, p. 116.

15. HARRIS, J. L. *Subject Headings: Factors Influencing Formation and Choice; With Special Reference to Library of Congress and H. W. Wilson Practice*. New York, Columbia University, 1969. (Ph.D. thesis) p. 59.

16. op. cit., p. 65.

17. SHELL, E.E. "A Rationale for Using the Library of Congress System in Re-classification. *In*: *Re-classification; rationale and problems. Proc. of a conference* . . . College Park, School of Library and Information Services, University of Maryland, 1968. p. 41.

18. *Report of the Librarian of Congress for the Fiscal Year ending June 30, 1916*. p. 103.

19. DAY, D.A. "Accuracy and Utility of Subject-related Responses." *In*: University of Chicago. Graduate Library School. *Requirements Study for Future Catalogs*. Progress report no. 2. Chicago, 1968. p. 57.

20. NEVILLE, H.H. "Feasibility Study of a Scheme for Reconciling Thesauri Covering a Common Subject." *Journal of Documentation*, v. 26, no. 4, Dec. 1970, p. 313-336.

21. ENGINEERS' JOINT COUNCIL. *Thesaurus of Engineering and Scientific Terms*. New York, 1967.

22. U. S. OFFICE OF WATER RESOURCES RESEARCH. *Water Resources Thesaurus*. Washington, 1966.

23. Op. cit., p. 314.

24. AITCHISON, JEAN, et al. *Thesaurofacet: a Thesaurus and Faceted Classification for Engineering and Related Subjects*. Whetstone, English Electric Co., 1970.

25. BORKO, H. "Subject Analysis from a Communications Point of View." Paper presented at the A.L.A. Preconference on Subject Analysis of Library Materials, Atlantic City, N.J., 1969.

26. RICHMOND, P.A. "LC and Dewey: their Relevance to Modern Information needs." Paper presented at the A.L.A. Preconference on Subject Analysis of Library Materials, Atlantic City, N.J., 1969.

27. *INTREX: Report of a Planning Conference on Information Transfer Experiments,* 1965. Edited by C.F.J. Overhage and R. J. Harman. Cambridge, Mass., MIT Press, 1965.
28. GOODMAN, N. "About." *Mind,* v. 70, no. 277, Jan. 1961, p. 1-24.
29. PUTNAM, H. "Formalization of the Concept 'About'." *Philosophy of Science,* v. 25, 1958. p. 125-130.
30. AUSTIN, D. "An Information Retrieval Language for MARC." *Aslib Proc.,* v. 22, no. 10, Oct. 1970, p. 481-491.
31. WOOSTER, H. *Towards a Uniform Federal Report Numbering System and a Cuddly Microfiche Reader—Two Modest Proposals.* Springfield, Va., Clearinghouse for Federal Scientific and Technical Information, 1968. (AD-669204)
32. LINE, M.B. "On the Design of Information Systems for Human Beings." *Aslib Proc.,* v. 22, July 1970, p. 320-335.
33. SWANSON, R. "The Information Business Is a People Business." *Information Storage and Retrieval,* v. 6, no. 4, Oct. 1970, p. 351-361.

•

DISCUSSION

Mr. *Jackson* felt that Mr. Wellisch had emphasized the defects of the LC subject headings disproportionately and said that he had always had sympathetic responses from the Library of Congress in his challenges to it. In the matter of the need for more money for the Library he noted that this was only one side of the problem: skilled manpower was also necessary, and, even if both were available, improvement of the subject heading list would still have to take its place in the Library's list of priorities. So far as the users of academic libraries were concerned, he did not believe that they thought that they were getting everything possible out of the collection simply by consulting the catalog.

Mr. *Wellisch* replied that his intention had not been to pick on individual headings except to emphasize the lack of any underlying system: no one could ever be sure how to construct a new subject heading, nor how to revise an existing heading. Furthermore, no user of a catalog could ever outguess the maker of the subject heading when trying to locate information.

Mr. *Spalding* regretted that Mr. Angell's paper, describing the current situation and future plans for the Library of Congress subject headings, had not taken precedence over Mr. Wellisch's paper in the Symposium program.

RECENT RESEARCH TRENDS IN THE FIELD OF INFORMATION RETRIEVAL LANGUAGES

by Eric de Grolier

Instituts Universitaires de Technologie
Tours, France

(The following text is an edited version of a tape transcript.)

In discussing research trends in the field of information retrieval languages we must first define what we mean by the term and, since there is no clear, internationally standardized definition I will adopt that given by J.-C. Gardin: any set of symbols used for expressing certain characteristics of data on which data processing is performed, in whatever field. Gardin adds that the data are frequently verbal data and, in this case, what is envisaged is the data from the point of view of meaning or content. Generally these languages are organized on the paradigmatic plane, i.e. they are presented in the form of a classification system. Furthermore, these languages are often accompanied by rules which determine the permitted syntactic links, or, in other words, they possess some form of organization on the syntagmatic plane. In 1967, Gardin introduced a differentiation which is now generally adopted in France: he said that information retrieval languages are part of the larger class of semantic meta-languages oriented towards applications in the field of retrieval of scientific and technical information. This definition, therefore, excludes meta-languages which are constructed to describe objects, for example archeological objects.

Some idea of the historical background to information retrieval and the emergence of principles is also essential for an understanding of recent developments. The first of these principles, the principle of specific entry, was discovered by C. A. Cutter and a little later Wyndham Hulme enunciated the principle of literary warrant which had already been put into effect by the Library of Congress in making its classification scheme. Even earlier Melvil Dewey had invented a principle which the Bibliothèque Nationale in Paris had been striving to achieve for over two centuries, that is the principle of the independence of classification and notation. Dewey was also responsible for the principle of common subdivisions, at least in its earliest formulation, but this was more properly the discovery of Paul Otlet in 1895, and later of J. D. Brown in Britain. The principles enunciated so far may be termed the "first round" and there is rather a long span of time between this first round of principles and the second round.

One of the most important of this second round of principles was the recognition that natural classifications, i.e. classification systems which conform to what Bliss called the "natural order of things", are not tree structures but lattices. This was discovered very early, but not in the field of book classification, by the French mathematician Cournot in 1851 and again by the English mathematician, physicist and linguist, Dyer. In our own field, Otlet was a precursor, but the real discovery was made by Desaubliaux and Cordonnier in 1943, and by Fairthorne and, independently, Mooers about five years later. Another important transfer from another field was the recognition of what in linguistics had been called paradigmatic and syntagmatic relations. This idea was applied to information retrieval languages in the 1950's by Perry and Kent. Then, another principle was that there are many kinds of analytical relations; not only inclusion or genus/species, but also part/whole, agent/process, process/property and agent/action relationships, as well as others. Subsequently there was Farradane's work on synthetic relations, followed by Kervégant in France and Perreault in the U.S.A.

If we now ask, "What are the principle discoveries in recent years?", we will find five things. The first is the definition of the field. No science can be well-formed if it does not have a well-defined object and it must be said that the definition of the object, information retrieval language, was not clear until about five years ago. There was opposition between various methods and various minds and the realization of their common properties and their common features was very difficult to achieve because of vested interests in particular systems.

The second point is that one must have a unified terminology and this terminology does not exist even now. Almost every author has his own terminology and to reconcile these terminologies and to say what is hidden behind the various terms which have been adopted is not an easy thing. So in this respect we have no science: we are in the situation of chemistry before Lavoisier or physics before Newton.

Thirdly, a science should have a good, logical typology, and neither does this exist as yet. One of the first was that of Holmstrom in 1948, then Jonker produced an extremely bad one in 1958, followed by another bad one by Coyaud in 1964 which provoked Gardin to make a much better one in 1966. There have been others, for example by Toman, by Ranganathan, and by Gilchrist, and the curious fact is that everyone of these taxonomists totally ignored the work of their predecessors. Hence, one of the research necessities in our field is a good typology.

The fourth point is the objective study of performance of existing systems, of so-called information retrieval language efficiency. This was begun by Cleverdon, in an experimental environment, 13 years ago and in relation to real systems in real environments by Lancaster in his work on MEDLARS only recently, at least as far as automated systems are concerned. In fact, in the USA, Grace Kelley had studied conventional systems as early as 1936, but her work, which is really a masterpiece, is now totally ignored.

The fifth necessity is experimental work on new systems, on new components of systems, and this was begun almost simultaneously in the United States by Salton, first at Harvard and then at Cornell; in France by Gardin and his team; and also in the USSR.

Now, if we consider these five conditions for research we can say that it is only within the past four or five years that these conditions have become more or less fulfilled. The curious thing is that almost simultaneously with the fulfillment of the conditions it began to be suggested that information retrieval languages were a thing of the past and that they had been replaced by the mechanized searching of natural language. To my mind, this idea was completely demolished by Gardin in a series of articles over the last three or four years. However, it is one thing to demolish a theory and quite another to demolish a practice, and the practice is now more alive than ever because of the simple fact that the computer is able to deal with natural language phrases by well-established KWIC, KWOC and SLIC programs.

One must also pay some attention to the "planes" upon which information retrieval languages may be considered, and here Ranganathan usefully distinguished three planes: the idea plane, the verbal plane, and the notational plane. We may alternatively describe these as the plane of logic, the plane of linguistics, and the plane of semiotics.

On the logical plane we consider the various ways of organizing concepts and here a great deal of work has been done, mainly by nondocumentalists such as Piaget whose so-called genetic psychology is relevant in this respect. An associated field is that of the social organization of science, in which Robert K. Merton was a pioneer and to which contributions have been made by de Solla Price and Kuhn. Recently related problems in the field of the social sciences have been discussed in *Social Science Information* by Levi-Strauss, Jacobson, Piaget, Galtung and Moscovici. Then it is important also to consider the history of the organization of knowledge: it is important to see how a consensus has evolved and how the organization of the sciences has been conceived. The names Wundt, Ostwald, Flint and Bliss are significant in this respect and others have studied the influence of the organization of knowledge on the organization of libraries and bibliographies and information retrieval systems, for example, Petzholdt, Bliss again, and de Grolier. These studies have shown that the concepts of static knowledge and slow evolution have been replaced by the concept of sudden revolutions in the structure of knowledge: revolutions which have made the old classification systems completely outmoded from the point of view of the scientist. An instance of this was the decision of the American Institute of Physics, having spent a great deal of National Science Foundation money in experiments on the mechanization of UDC, to drop the entire project on the grounds that UDC had been developed before the quanta and relativity revolution and that it was therefore impossible to use in a system for physics information retrieval.

On the linguistic plane, much work has been done, again by non-documentalists, by anthropologists for example, in their studies of the semantic structure of kinship which is equivalent to the study of semantic factors carried out by Perry and Kent in relation to information retrieval languages. The semantic field is also of importance on the linguistic plane but its application to the field of information retrieval languages has been at a very primitive level. So far as syntactic structures are concerned, however, the situation is brighter with some excellent work having been done by Borillo in France.

We have seen from mathematics that the notational, or semiotic, plane is extremely significant but there is insufficient time to pursue that topic here. One may, however, cite the work of Vickery and Foskett in England and of Cordonnier in France.

In addition to the three planes described above there are other topics which deserve some attention. Firstly, there is the matter of how people judge relevance or pertinency: there was a great deal of fuss about this subject before Cuadra discovered the very simple fact that relevance is a psychological fact which has to be investigated by psycho-sociological methods before it can be used intelligently in evaluation studies.

Secondly, it is necessary to remind ourselves that the science of information retrieval languages must proceed with models as every science does and we have had several of these, the earliest being that of Kaiser in 1911, then Fairthorne in 1948, Ranganathan with his postulates between 1947 and the present day, and, most recently, that of Gardin. None of these models is entirely satisfactory and the best evidence for this is our presence at this symposium.

Finally, there are a number of unsolved problems which deserve mention. Firstly, there is the debate over the possibility of a universal system between two totally antagonistic schools of thought; secondly, and related to the first, there is the problem of compatibility between systems; thirdly, there is the question of whether or not systems should be based upon disciplines; and, finally, there is the big question of the possibility of mechanical translation applied to information retrieval systems; that is, the mechanical translation of natural languages to one or more information retrieval languages, a field in which research is just beginning—perhaps a conference should be organized at Maryland in 1980 to discuss this problem!

DISCUSSION

Mr. *Wellisch* asked if Mr. de Grolier could give some examples of the typologies to which he had referred.

M. *de Grolier* noted that the early typologies were extremely crude, for example that of Jonker was based upon only one characteristic — the length of the descriptor — and he made a number of false assumptions, for example: that hierarchical classifications systems index by the longest possible terms; that classification systems do not use more than two indexing criteria; that you cannot obtain greater hierarchical definition and at the same time increase recall.

Gardin's typology of 1966 distinguished between natural and documentary lexica and, in the latter category, distinguished between those which make explicit the correspondence between natural language and information retrieval languages (i.e. thesauri) and the rest, which leave this correspondence implicit (i.e. unorganized alphabetic lists, and organized lists such as classification schemes and subject heading lists). He then further divided the organized lists into mono-dimensional and multi-dimensional systems and said that, generally speaking, they are multidimensional and have a means for expressing analytic relations, and sometime also syntactic relations. Such systems could be set on a continuum with hierarchical or quasi-hierarchical systems which use a strict semantic order at one end, and, at the other end, faceted classification systems with exclusively syntactic organization. Gardin adds that one may have in any of these systems univocal or multivocal organization, i.e. systems in which a term appears only once, and those in which a term may appear many times.

A typology such as this, said M. *de Grolier,* is artificial, putting very different systems in the same class and analogous systems in different classes.

Further discussion ensued on the point of the vocabulary of information science and M. *de Grolier* noted that progress in other fields had taken place before the vocabulary of those fields was fully organized but that, nevertheless, an attempt to control the use of words in any field was desirable.

Mr. *Freeman* commented that he had retrieved from his files the original research proposal from the American Institute of Physics and that it was obvious that there was no intention on the part of AIP to adopt UDC for any of its operations—it was purely a research project.

REFERENCES

(This list of references has been prepared by one of the editors (T.D.W.) to accompany M. de Grolier's paper. For this reason it is likely to include some items that M. de Grolier would not have included, and to exclude others which he would have included.)

BELY, N. *Procedures d'analyse semantique appliquées à la documentation scientifique,* par N. Bely, A. Borillo, Jacques Virbel et N. Siot-Decauville. Paris, Gauthier-Villars, 1970.

BLISS, H.E. *Organization of Knowledge in Libraries.* 2nd ed. New York, H.W. Wilson, 1939.

BLISS, H.E. *Organization of Knowledge and the System' of the Sciences.* New York, Holt, 1929.

BROWN, J.D. *Subject Classification.* 3rd ed. Revised by J.D. Stewart. London, Grafton, 1939.

CLEVERDON, C.W. *Factors Determining the Performance of Indexing Systems.* Cranfield, Aslib-Cranfield Research Project, 1966.

CLEVERDON, C.W. *Report on the Testing and Analysis of an Investigation into the Comparative Efficiency of Indexing Systems.* Cranfield, Aslib-Cranfield Research Project, 1962.

CORDONNIER, G. "Méthodes nouvelles de documentation." *Comité national de l'organisation française* v.25, nos. 4-6, 1951.

CORDONNIER, G. "A new method of syllabic coding", in *Classification Research: Proceedings of the Second International Study Conference . . . 1964* Edited by Pauline Atherton. Copenhagen, Munksgaard, 1965. p.121-130.

COURNOT, A.A. *Essai sur les fondements de nos connaissances et sur les caractères de la critique philosophique.* Paris, Hachette, 1851.

COYAUD, M. *Introduction a l'étude des langages documentaires.* Paris, Klincksieck, 1966.

CUADRA, C.A. and KATTER, R.V. "Opening the Black Box of Relevance" *Journal of Documentation* v.23, no.4, December 1967, p.291-303.

CUTTER, C.A. *Rules for a Dictionary Catalog.* 4th ed. Washington, U.S. Bureau of Education, 1904.

DESAUBLIAUX, R. *Le danger des classifications linéaires appliquées aux problèmes sociaux et économiques.* Paris, Bernard, 1943.

FAIRTHORNE, R.A. *Towards Information Retrieval.* London, Butterworths, 1961.

FARRADANE, J.E.L. "Relational Indexing" *The Indexer* v.2, no.4, Autumn 1961, p.127-133.

FARRADANE, J.E.L. "The Psychology of Classification" *Journal of Documentation* v.11, no.4, December 1955, p.187-201.

FLINT, R. *Philosophy as Scientia Scientiarum and a History of Classifications of the Sciences.* London, W. Blackwood & Sons, 1904.

FOSKETT, D.J. *Classification and Indexing in the Social Sciences.* London, Butterworths, 1963.

GARDIN, J.-C. "Eléments d'un modèle pour la description des lexiques documentaires" *Bulletin des Bibliothèques de France* v.11, no.5, mai 1966. p.171-182.

GARDIN, J.-C. *SYNTOL.* Rutgers, the State University, 1965.

GROLIER, E. de *A study of General Categories Applicable to Classification and Coding in Documentation.* Paris, Unesco, 1962.

GROLIER, E. de *Théorie et pratique des classifications documentaires.* Paris, UFOD, 1956.

HOLMSTROM, J.E. "A Classification of Classifications", *in F.I.D. Conference, Berne, 1947: Conference reports* v.1, p.29-36. (F.I.D. Report No. 17)

HULME, E.W. *Principles of Book Classification.* London, Association of Assistant Librarians, 1950. (A.A.L. Reprints Series)

JONKER, F. *Indexing Theory, Indexing Methods and Search Devices.* New York, Scarecrow Press, 1964.

KAISER, J. *Systematiç Indexing.* London, Pitman, 1911

KELLEY, G.O. *The Classification of Books.* New York, H.W. Wilson, 1937.

KERVEGANT, D. "Classification et analyse des relations" *Bulletin des Bibliothèques de France* v.4, no.11, novembre 1959, p.495-511.

KUHN, T.S. *The Structure of Scientific Revolutions.* Chicago, University of Chicago Press, 1962.

LANCASTER, F.W. *Evaluation of the MEDLARS Demand Search Service.* Washington, National Library of Medicine, 1968.

MERTON, R.K. *Science, Technology and Society in Seventeenth Century England.* New York, H. Fertig, 1970.

MERTON, R.K. *Social Theory and Social Structure.* Glencoe, Free Press, 1957.

MERTON, R.K. "The Matthew Effect in Science" *Science* v.159, January 5, 1968, p.56-63.

MOOERS, C.N. "A Mathematical Theory of the Use of Language Symbols in Retrieval", *in Proceedings of the International Conference on Scientific Information, Washington, December, 1958.* Washington, National Academy of Sciences - National Research Council, 1959. Vol.2, p.1327-1364.

OTLET, P. *Traité de documentation.* Brussels, Editions Mundaneum, 1934.

PERREAULT, J.M. "Categories and Relations: A New Schema" *Revue Internationale de Documentation* v.32, no.4, 1965, p.136-144.

PERRY, J.W. and KENT, A. *Tools for Machine Literature Searching.* New York, Interscience, 1958.

PETZHOLDT, J. *Bibliotheca bibliographica.* Nieuwkoop, B. de Graaf, 1961. (Reprint of 1866 edition)

PIAGET, J. *Introduction à l'epistemologie génétique.* Paris, Presses Universitaires, 1950.

PIAGET, J. *The Mechanisms of Perception.* New York, Basic Books, 1969.

PRICE, D.J. de S. *Little Science, Big Science.* New Haven, Yale University Press, 1963.

PRICE, D.J. de S. "Networks of Scientific Papers" *Science* v.149, 1965, p.510-515.

PRICE, D.J. de S. *Science Since Babylon.* New Haven, Yale University Press, 1961.

RANGANATHAN, S.R. *Prolegomena to Library Classification.* 3rd ed. New York, Asia Publishing House, 1967.

SALTON, G. *Automatic Information Organization and Retrieval.* New York, McGraw-Hill, 1968.

SAUSSURE, F. de *Course in General Linguistics.* New York, McGraw-Hill, 1959.

TOMAN, J. "The Influence of Information Retrieval on the Structure of Indexing and Classification Systems", *in Library Systems and Information Services: Proceedings of the Second Anglo-Czech Conference of Information Specialists, London, 1957.* Edited by D.J. Foskett, A. de Reuck, and H. Coblans. London, Crosby Lockwood, 1970. p.57-66.

VICKERY, B.C. *Classification and Indexing in Science.* 2nd ed. London, Butterworths, 1959.

WUNDT, W. *System der Philosophie.* Leipzig, Engelmann, 1889.

YNGVE, W.H. "In Defense of English", *in Information Retrieval and Machine Translation.* New York, Interscience, 1960. Chapter 40.

A GENERAL MODEL FOR INDEXING LANGUAGES: THE BASIS FOR COMPATIBILITY AND INTEGRATION

Dagobert Soergel

School of Library and Information Services
University of Maryland

Classification theory is divided into two areas: analysis of conceptual structure and file organization. The primacy of the first is stressed. A model for conceptual structure in terms of concept coordination and polyhierarchy is sketched. Some problems of file organization, namely post-coordination vs. pre-coordination and synthetic vs. enumerative schemes are discussed in relation to this model. A model for a classification scheme for different kinds of file organization is then proposed. The scheme would consist of a "core classification scheme" made up of elemental concepts and an "extended classification scheme" made up of combinations of elemental concepts. While the core scheme would be universal, extended schemes would be developed as needed in a specific application. This would make for flexibility while maintaining inter-system compatibility.

0 Introduction

The purpose of this paper is to give a perspective, not new results. It tries to put into perspective the problems of classification theory. These problems can be divided into two major areas: conceptual structure and file organization. It seems to this writer that classificationists have concentrated too exclusively on file organization and have looked too often on conceptual structure from the point of view of file organization and not as an area to be considered independently. This imposed many restrictions on the consideration of conceptual structure, and many aspects important for information retrieval have not been brought out. This might be one of the reasons why the results of classification theory have been neglected or sometimes reinvented in a rather amateurish manner in mechanized information retrieval systems where the restrictions imposed by file organization are by far less severe than in manual systems.

Contrary to this attitude we take the following position: the primary and basic task is to understand conceptual structure and its functions in the retrieval process. We say again that this task should be performed

36

without any reference to the limitations imposed by any particular kind of file organization. File organization is the secondary, technical, almost ancillary task. File organization has to put into effect the insights gained from the analysis of conceptual structure for actual application in performing searches as far as is feasible with the equipment available in the particular system. It should be obvious that problems like pre-coordination and post-coordination, synthetic vs. enumerative schemes or alphabetical vs. classified order are problems of file organization. Whatever the file organization is, it should be based on the came conceptual structure. As we shall see later, this will increase considerably the effectiveness of information retrieval systems. Furthermore, this principle would serve to maintain compatibility between information retrieval systems with different kinds of file organization, e.g. a file of optical coincidence cards (popularly known as "peek-a-boo" cards) or a conventional card catalogue.

1. *Conceptual structure: concept coordination and hierarchy*

1.1 *Hierarchy*

Due to schemes like the Dewey Decimal Classification (DC), the Universal Decimal Classification (UDC) and the Library of Congress Classification (LC) misconceptions of hierarchy are widespread. Hierarchy is *not* a strait jacket in which the universe of knowledge has to fit somehow or other. On the contrary, a properly designed hierarchy is a device to assist in indexing documents and in performing searches for documents or other retrieval objects. Whenever a hierarchy sets constraints, it is faulty; whenever it helps the indexer or searcher, it serves its functions.

Based on this practical attitude to hierarchy we define hierarchical relationships as follows:

Concept A is *broader than* concept B, whenever the following holds:

In any search for A all items dealing with B should be found. (A less rigorous and more practical formulation would be: In most searches for A most items dealing with B should be found.)

Given a set of concepts, the traditional approach to hierarchy building is to subdivide this set into mutually exclusive groups, to subdivide in turn each of these groups into mutually exclusive subgroups, and so on. The emphasis is on putting the concepts into some kind of orderly arrangement. If a concept does not fit "naturally" into that arrangement, it is arbitrarily put somewhere. If, on the other hand, a concept would fit into different places, it is more or less arbitrarily assigned to one of them: no concept is allowed to have more than one broader concept. This principle we call mono-hierarchy. It is quite obvious, especially in the light of our above definition, that this approach is artificial and imposes many constraints.

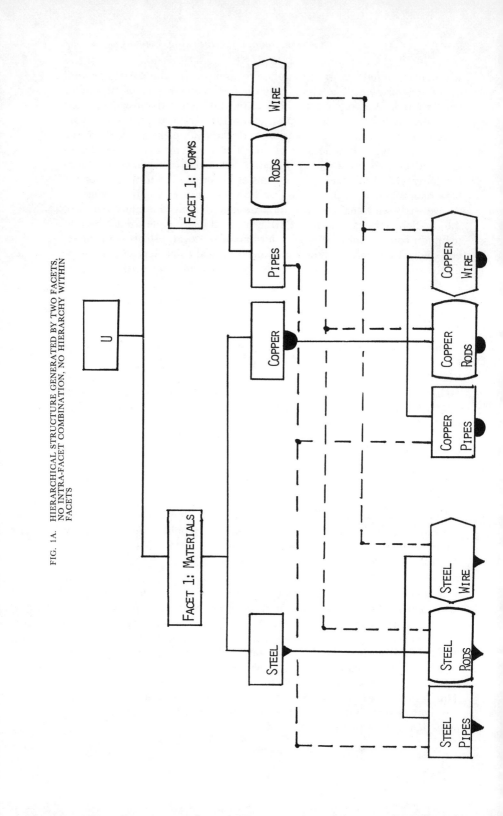

FIG. 1A.   HIERARCHICAL STRUCTURE GENERATED BY TWO FACETS, NO INTRA-FACET COMBINATION, NO HIERARCHY WITHIN FACETS

FIG. 1B. DIFFERENT POSSIBLE LINEAR ARRANGEMENTS OF THE
CONCEPTS GIVEN IN FIG. 1A.

"Ruly" arrangement 1

1 Steel

2 Steel pipes → 9

3 Steel rods → 10

4 Steel wire → 11

5 Copper

6 Copper pipes → 9

7 Copper rods → 10

8 Copper wire → 11

9 Pipes → 2,6

10 Rods → 3,7

11 Wire → 4,8

"Ruly" arrangement 2

1 Steel → 4,7,10

2 Copper → 5,8,11

3 Pipes

4 Steel pipes → 1

5 Copper pipes → 2

6 Rods

7 Steel rods → 1

8 Copper rods → 2

9 Wire

10 Steel wire → 1

11 Copper wire → 2

Arbitrary arrangement 1

1 Steel → 11

2 Steel pipes → 6

3 Steel rods → 8

4 Copper → 7,9

5 Copper wire → 10

6 Pipes → 2

7 Copper pipes → 4

8 Rods → 3

9 Copper rods → 4

10 Wire → 5

11 Steel wire → 1

(Less) arbitrary arrangement 2

1 Steel

2 Steel pipes → 6

3 Steel rods → 8

4 Steel wire → 10

5 Copper → 7,9,11

6 Pipes → 2

7 Copper pipes → 5

8 Rods → 3

9 Copper rods → 5

10 Wire → 4

11 Copper wire → 5

The modern approach is quite different. Any two concepts are analyzed as to whether or not the condition in the above definition holds for them. If the answer is yes, a hierarchical relationship is established between the two concepts. If not, no such relationship is established. While some concepts may end up with having only one broader concept, others might have two or more. Examples:

Constitution	broader concepts:	Politics
		Public law
Social psychology	broader concepts:	Sociology
		Psychology
Railroad stations	broader concepts:	Railroads
		Stations

This we call poly-hierarchy.

On the other hand it may turn out that the application of this procedure leaves a concept without any broader concept at all. These concepts on top of the hierarchy may be broad subject fields such as Economics. But they may also be specific concepts which happen to have no broader concepts, such as "Packaging" (in DC there is no number for this concept as a whole) or "Weights and measures" (wrongly placed under 380 *Commerce* in DC).

Having introduced all hierarchical relationships that are useful for the search process, one should of course try to bring the concepts into an orderly arrangement which expresses as many of the hierarchical relationships as possible. Hierarchical relationships not expressed by the arrangement have to be expressed by cross-references. We shall come back to this problem later.

1.2 *Concept coordination*

It is well known that by combination of concepts more compound concepts can be formed. The reverse of this process is to break down or factor compound concepts into less compound concepts. First of all, the breakdown into semantic factors is useful for the detection of structural relationships between concepts, as we shall see shortly. This is the aspect which interests us in this section. Secondly, semantic factoring may be used to achieve economy of the searching devices in mechanized retrieval systems (such as peek-a-boo systems or computerized systems).

A word of caution is in order: We are *not* concerned with the linguistic decomposition of multi-word or compound terms, but with the semantic factoring of concepts according to their meaning. Thus, for example, "gross national product" is a multi-word term designating a concept, the breakdown of which is not useful. On the other hand, the term "ship",

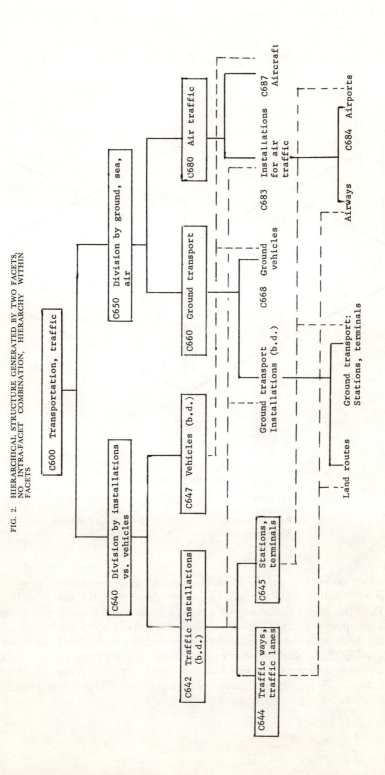

FIG. 2. HIERARCHICAL STRUCTURE GENERATED BY TWO FACETS, NO INTRA-FACET COMBINATION, HIERARCHY WITHIN FACETS

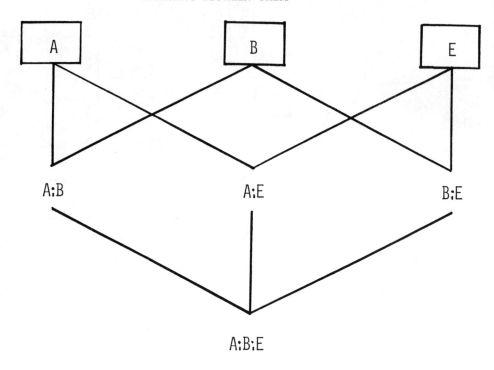

FIGURE 3. HIERARCHICAL STRUCTURE GENERATED BY 3 GEN-
ERATING CONCEPTS WITHOUT HIERARCHICAL RELA-
TIONSHIPS BETWEEN THEM

Generating concepts:

A Vehicles   E United States
B Ground transport   F France
C Rail transport   G Great Britain
D Road transport

which is simple from the linguistic point of view, designates a compound
concept which may usefully be broken down into the semantic factors
Vehicles: Water transport. Of course, a multi-word term often designates
a compound concept. In some cases, the conceptual semantic factoring
coincides with the linguistic decomposition, for example: *Lead pipes* =
Lead : Pipes. But by no means does this apply in every case. To cite
an extreme example: *White House* = *Agency : Chief executive : United
States.* ("White House" here used in the sense "The White House an-
nounces . . .").

FIGURE 4. HIERARCHICAL STRUCTURE GENERATED BY 5 GEN-
ERALIZING CONCEPTS WITH HIERARCHICAL RELATION-
SHIPS BETWEEN THEM

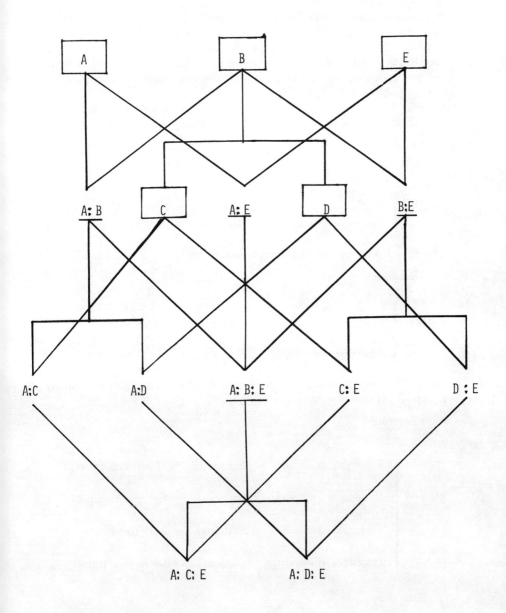

1.3 *Interaction of concept coordination and hierarchy*

In the early days of coordinate indexing it was suggested (and this is still a widespread opinion) that semantic factoring on the one hand and hierarchy on the other are opposite principles and that systems are either based on coordinate indexing or on hierarchical classification schemes. A simple example suffices to reveal the superficiality of this opinion: *Railroad stations* may be broken down into *Railroads : Stations*. However, the concepts *Railroads* and *Stations* are both broader than *Railroad stations*. This is a simple example showing the interaction of concept coordination and hierarchy. In general, the following rules, familiar from the process of broadening or narrowing down a search request, hold:

Starting from a concept A:B:C one may arrive at *broader concepts* by (1) Dropping one of the components (dropping a restriction).

Example:

	A	B	C
	Passenger transport:	Stations	
broader ↑	A	B	C
	Passenger transport:	Stations:	Local rail transit

(2) Broadening one of the components (weakening a restriction).

Example:

	A	B	C^1
broader ↑	Passenger transport:	Stations:	Rail transport
	A	B	C
	Passenger transport:	Stations:	Local rail transit

If one weakens a restriction more and more, the restriction is finally dropped: (1) is a special case of (2).

Example:

	A	B	C^{111}
	Passenger transport:	Stations:	(Universal concept)
	A	B	C^{11}
broader ↑	Passenger transport:	Stations:	Ground transport
	A	B	C^1
	Passenger transport:	Stations:	Rail transport
	A	B	C
	Passenger transport:	Stations:	Local rail transit

The rules for forming *narrower concepts* are the exact opposite of those for broader concepts. There is, however, a third possibility:

(3) There may be concepts narrower than A:B which *cannot* be derived by any of these methods.

Example:
Helicopter is narrower than *Vehicles: Air traffic* but cannot be derived by adding a useful semantic factor.

Fig. 1 - 4 show hierarchical structures generated by these rules.

In summary, we may say:

Semantic factoring or concept coordination on the one hand and hierarchy on the other are not opposite and mutually exclusive principles. On the contrary, they interact with each other.

This finishes our study of conceptual structure. We can now go on to problems of file organization.

2. File Organization for Retrieval

As we said before, problems such as pre-coordination vs. post-coordination, enumerative vs. synthetic schemes and alphabetical vs. classified arrangement are problems of file organization. We shall look at these problems from a somewhat different point of view which will lead us to somewhat different and more refined distinctions.

2.0 The problem defined

The problem to be solved by file organization may simply be stated as follows: Documents deal with compound concepts, made up of many components and called *document delineation*.

Example:
The Glideway system, a high-speed ground transportation system in the northeastern United States.

Components of compound concept (document delineation):
Traffic networks; Traffic modelling and simulation; Traffic ways; Stations; Vehicles; Propulsion of vehicles; Rail transport; High-speed transport; Schedules; Passenger traffic; United States.

Searches are also made for compound concepts, called search request formulation, but these search concepts are usually made up of fewer components.

Examples:

(1) Stations for rail transport.

Components of compound concept (search request formulation):
Stations: Rail transport

FIGURE 5. DOCUMENT DELINEATIONS IN DIFFERENT FILE SYSTEMS

Title:

The Glideway system, a high-speed ground transportation system in the northeastern United States.

(a) *Document delineation in a peek-a-boo system* (many elemental concepts):

Traffic networks; Traffic modelling and simulation; Traffic ways; Stations, terminals; Vehicles; Propulsion of vehicles; Rail transport; High-speed transport; Schedules; Passenger traffic; United States

(c) *Document delineation in a card catalog* (few compound concepts):

Passenger transportation networks
Rail transport stations
Rail transport vehicles - high speed

(b) *Document delineation in a shelving system* (one very compound concept):

High speed rail transportation networks for passenger transport.

(2) A regional network for passenger transport in the northeastern United States.

Components of compound concept (search request formulation):
Transportation network: Passenger transport: United States

The problem is, then, to retrieve those documents the delineation of which is equal to or narrower than the search request formulation. (In the case of non-inclusive searches, one wishes to retrieve only those documents with a document delineation equal to the search request formulation.) We shall discuss several possibilities to solve this problem, that is, several possibilities of file organization. We shall confine ourselves in this discussion to inverted files. We shall call "entry-concepts" those concepts under which entries are made in the inverted file. An entry is defined here in a more general way; it may be a document number or call number or a condensed document description such as on a catalogue card, or the full text of a document, stored on shelves or in a computer, etc.

FIG. 6. CONCEPT NARROWER DUE TO COMBINATION VS. CONCEPT NARROWER DUE TO SUBSTITUTION

Search request formulation:

A			B	
Vehicles:			Rail transport	

Document delineation:

A	B	C	A	B′
Vehicles:	Rail transport:	Passenger transport	Vehicles:	Local rail transit

Narrower due to combination

Retrieved by searching in coordinate indexing systems (Peek-a-boo, computers, etc.)

Narrower due to B′ substitution

B′ Local rail transit is narrower than B Rail transport.
In order that a document on A:B may be retrieved, "Generic posting" from B′ to B has to be introduced.

2.1 *Principal solutions: post-coordination vs. pre-coordination—a quantitative view*

2.1.1 The most important parameter in characterizing file organization in our context is the degree of compoundness of the entry concepts. This is a "quantitative" version of the dichotomy post-coordination vs. pre-coordination.

(a) At the one end of the scale we have files where the entry concepts are elemental or at least of a very low degree of compoundness. The usual application of peek-a-boo cards would be a concrete example. The number of entry concepts in these files is comparatively small. A document delineation (the compound concept assigned to a document) is made by listing many of the elemental or nearly elemental concepts (see figure 5a); an entry is made under each of these elemental concepts (multiple entry with numerous entries). In the same way, a search request formulation is made up as a combination of elemental or nearly elemental concepts, which may easily be found in the comparatively small list of entry concepts. A search for this combination is then made; this type of file is useful only in the case where it is feasible, from a mechanical point of view, to search for combinations of entry concepts, such as in the case of coordinated indexing systems (e.g. peek-a-boo cards or computerized files). All documents are retrieved that have delineations equal to or narrower than the search request formulation due to combination. By "narrower due to combination" we mean A:B:C being narrower than

A:B. As we have seen, this is to be distinguished from A:B' being narrower than B. If, in a coordinated indexing system, documents on A:B' are also to be retrieved, generic posting from B' to B has to be introduced. (See fig. 6).

(b) On the other end of the scale we have files which use very compound entry concepts, such as files where documents are arranged on shelves by subject. In this case, we have a huge number of entry concepts. A document delineation is made up of one very compound concept (see figure 5b); only one entry is made (single entry). In preparing a search, the first step is to find among the huge number of very compound entry concepts the one which is equal to the search request formulation; for an inclusive search, one has to find in addition all those which are narrower than the search request formulation. In a second step, one can then retrieve the documents entered under these concepts. We shall come back shortly to the important problem of how to find the appropriate compound entry concepts.

(c) In the middle of the scale we have files using moderately compound entry concepts, such as in subject heading catalogues. The number of entry concepts is large, but not as large as in (b). A document delineation is made up of a few subject headings (see figure 5c); an entry is made for each of these (multiple entry with a few entries). In preparing a search, one has first to find the appropriate subject headings from among the large number of subject headings; this poses problems similar to, but less severe, than finding the very compound entry concepts in (b). In a second step, one can then scan the entries under one of those subject headings to retrieve the pertinent documents. If it is mechanically feasible, one might also search immediately for a combination of subject headings.

2.1.2 Remark: We have linked in this discussion the degree of compoundness of the entry concepts and the number of entries made for a document in spite of the fact that these two parameters are in principle independent from each other. The linkage set forth here holds if one starts from the requirement that the document delineation be of the same degree of precision with every type of file organization. In actual systems the degree of compoundness increases less than the number of entries decreases. As a result, the delineations of the documents become less precise (see figure 5).

2.1.3 After this digression we come back to what is the basic problem of this paper. We have seen that in systems using compound entry concepts the problem arises of finding the appropriate entry concepts for indexing or searching among the large number of entry concepts. It follows that a mechanism for the retrieval of the appropriate compound entry concepts has to be provided. We could call this mechanism a secondary or auxiliary information retrieval system. Preempting the next section we may state already that it is here that the considerations of section 1 on conceptual structure come into play and are applied to "conventional" systems.

We could, for example, express the very compound entry concepts of a shelving classification by elemental concepts. To make this more concrete: we could make a catalog card for each compound entry concept. The compound concept would serve as "title". We could then write down the elemental concepts which in combination make up the compound.

Once this is done and the search request formulation is also expressed by elemental concepts, there is actually no substantial difference between retrieving documents the delineation of which is made up of elemental concepts, and retrieving compound entry concepts equal to or narrower than the search request formulation. The following illustration should clarify this point further:

In a file of newspaper clippings, the clippings are the documents; they are arranged in folders according to themes which are very compound concepts; that means, we have a shelving classification, the themes being the entry concepts, and we could set up a secondary information retrieval system to retrieve these themes. We could, for example, make up a catalog card for each theme, as discussed above. But we could also look at this file in another way: We could look at each folder as being a document, and at the theme of the folder as the delineation of that document in terms of elemental concepts. In this view, our catalog cards would stand for documents, the elemental concepts serving as indexing terms; our IR-system would become a primary IR-system, retrieving documents (namely the folders) and not a secondary IR-system, retrieving entry concepts.

In the majority of systems using compound entry concepts (with the notable exception of faceted classification) the auxiliary information retrieval system is rather weak (compare the remarks on LC subject headings in 2.2.1 and on LC and DC in 2.2.2).

We may summarize these considerations as follows:
Searching consists of two steps:

Step 1: Find the appropriate entry concepts to be used in the formulation of the search request.

Step 2: Retrieve documents by combination of the entry concepts found in step 1.

The "work load" of searching for the appropriate compound concepts may be distributed between the two steps. In a peek-a-boo file, entry concepts are elemental concepts, therefore no combination searching is necessary in step 1, and combination of many entry concepts takes place in step 2. In shelving classification, the entry concepts are very compound (ideally as compound as document descriptions); therefore there is combination searching involving many components in step 1, retrieving the appropriate entry concept (or concepts, in the case of inclusive searches), but there is no combination searching in step 2. Systems in between use moderately compound entry concepts so that both steps involve combination searching, with fewer components in each step.

We have already mentioned that the problems of file organization are much more difficult in systems using compound entry concepts than in systems using elemental or nearly elemental entry concepts, such as peek-a-boo systems. The rest of this paper concentrates on problems of systems using compound entry concepts (pre-coordinate systems). We shall first deal with the question how retrieval mechanisms for compound entry concepts can be designed. We shall then go on to the problems of selection of entry concepts and their arrangement in a file.

2.2 Retrieval mechanisms for entry concepts

In this section we are concerned with the retrieval of compound entry concepts in terms of their conceptual components (as specified for example in a search request). We are not at all concerned with alphabetical indexes where a compound concept may be found under the term used to designate it.

2.2.1 The first possibility for such a retrieval mechanism is to represent the poly-hierarchical structure formed by all the concepts in a linear arrangement with hierarchical cross-references (that means, "Broader Term" and "Narrower Term" cross references; these may be complemented by "Related Term" cross references, which are also useful for retrieving the appropriate entry concepts. In LC Subject Headings, all these are lumped together as "see also" cross references). If one chooses classified order, many hierarchical relationships can be expressed by the arrangement alone and cross-references are needed for the remaining ones only. If one chooses alphabetical order, all hierarchical relationships have to be expressed by cross-references. In principle, it is not necessary for this purpose that the compound concepts be expressed by semantic factors, as long as all hierarchical relationships are known. However, the task becomes much easier if one expresses the compound concepts by semantic factors, since the derivation of hierarchical relationships, the determination of the arrangement and the introduction of cross-references can then be done much more systematically and even be automated (See fig. 1B). (As to the arrangement, compare section 2.3(2), where this question is dealt with in detail.)

Someone looking for an entry concept appropriate for his indexing or searching purposes will enter the list at a broader concept which he knows. He will then go downwards in the classified arrangement,

FIG. 7. ILLUSTRATION OF A COMBINED INDEX TO LC SUBJECT
HEADINGS AND LC CLASSIFICATION ACCORDING TO 2.2.2

FIG. 7A. LC SUBJECT HEADINGS AND LC CLASS NUMBERS WITH
BREAKDOWN INTO SEMANTIC FACTORS

LC subject headings

Aeroplanes — Soundproofing	= Vehicles: Air transportation: Soundproofing
Airports — Buildings	= Buildings: Stations: Air transportation
Buildings — Soundproofing	= Buildings: Construction: Soundproofing
Ships — Soundproofing	= Vehicles: Water transportation: Soundproofing[1]

LC class numbers

HE 550-560	Ports, harbors, docks, wharves etc. = Stations: Water transportation: Civilian
NA 2800	Architectural acoustics = Architecture: Acoustics
NA 6300-6307	Airport buildings = Buildings: Stations: Air transportation: Civilian
NA 6330	Dock buildings, ferry houses etc. = Buildings: Stations: Water transportation: Civilian
TC 350-374	Harbor works = Stations: Water transportation: Engineering
TM 1725	Soundproof construction = Buildings: Construction: Soundproofing
TL 725-726	Airways (Routes), Airports, and landing Aerodromes[2] = Traffic installations: Air transportation
VA 67-79	Naval ports, bases, reservation, docks etc. = Stations: Water transportation: Military: US

1. There is no heading "Automobiles — Soundproofing".

2. It is not clear whether or not this class includes military airbases. Note that airports as such, which would have the component "Stations" instead of "Traffic installations", does not have its own LC class number.

FIG. 7B. "CORE CLASSIFICATION" (ELEMENTAL CONCEPTS NEEDED
TO GENERATE THE COMPOUND CONCEPTS IN FIG. 7A)

Vehicles

Traffic installations
        Stations, terminals

Air transportation
Water transportation

Buildings
Architecture
Construction
Engineering

Acoustics
        Soundproofing

Military
Civilian

US

NOTES:

1. It is easy to see that by using these elemental concepts many more compound
   concepts could be formed by combination than are given in Fig. 7a. In an
   actual situation, the number of elemental concepts needed is only a fraction
   of the original compound concepts.

2. In an actual situation, all the elemental concepts would form a polyhierarchical
   structure and be arranged in classified order, so that it would be easy to find
   the appropriate elemental concepts. A notation would then be assigned. In
   the index (Fig. 7c), concepts could be arranged according to their notation,
   so that for example "Acoustics" and "Soundproofing" would be collocated.

FIG. 7C. INDEX (KWIC - format)

Architecture:	Acoustics.	NA 2800
Buildings: Stations:	Air transportation.	Airports - Buildings
Traffic installations:	Air transportation.	TL 725 - 726
Buildings: Stations:	Air transportation: Civilian.	NA 6300-6307
: Vehicles	Air transportation: Soundproofing.	Aeroplanes - Soundproofing
	Architecture: Acoustics.	NA 2800
	Buildings: Construction: Soundproofing.	TM 1725; Buildings - Soundproofing
	Buildings: Stations: Air transpor	Airports - Buildings
	Buildings: Stations: Air transpor	NA 6300-6307
tation: Civilian.	Civilian.	NA 6330
tation: Civilian.	Civilian.	NA 6300-6307
ortation: Civilian.	Civilian.	NA 6330 .
	Construction: Soundproofing.	HE 550-560
	Engineering.	TM 1725; Buildings - Soundproofing
	Military: US.	TC 350-374
Stations: Air transportation:	Soundproofing.	VA 67-79
Stations: Water transportation:	Soundproofing.	TM 1725; Buildings - Soundproofing
Stations: Water transportation:	Soundproofing.	Aeroplanes - Soundproofing
Buildings:	Stations: Air transportation.	Ships - Soundproofing
Stations: Water transportation:	Stations: Air transportation.	Airports - Buildings
Stations: Water transportation:	Stations: Water transportation: Water transp	NA 6300-6307
Buildings: Construction:	Stations: Water transportation: Buildings	HE 550-560
Vehicles: Air transportation:	Stations: Water transportation: Buildings	NA 6330
Vehicles: Water transportation:	Stations: Water transportation:	TC 350-374
Buildings:	Traffic installations: Air transportation.	VA 67-79
Civilian. Buildings:	US. Stations	TL 725-726
Civilian.	Vehicles: Air transportation: Soundproofing.	VA 67-79
Civilian. Buildings:	Vehicles: Water transportation: Soundproof	Aeroplanes - Soundproofing
Engineering.	Water transportation: Civilian.	Ships - Soundproofing.
Military: US.	Water transportation: Civilian.	NA 6330
:Water transportation: Military:	Water transportation: Engineering.	HE 550-560
Buildings:	Water transportation: Military: US.	TC 350-374
Water transportation: Stations:	Water transportation: Soundproofing.	VA 67-79
Water transportation: Stations:		Ships - Soundproofing
Water transportation: Stations:		
Water transportation: Vehicles:		

Note: A sample search request might be: "Soundproofing of Vehicles"; this is expressed by the combination "Soundproofing": "Vehicles". One may enter the index under either term and scan the entries there for the other term. In this example one will find the two subject headings "Aeroplanes - Soundproofing" and "Ships-Soundproofing".

as well as following the cross-references, until he finds the appropriate entry concept.

We illustrate the process in a system where compound entry concepts are expressed by semantic factors. Someone has expressed his search concept by $A:B:C:E$. He enters the list at any of the components, say A. There he will look through the narrower concepts, either listed at the same place or indicated through cross-references. He will either find the entry concept he is looking for or he will find a broader concept, say $A:B:E$. In the latter case, he looks through the narrower concepts given for $A:B:E$, and there he finds $A:B:E:C$ (which, of course, is the same as $A:B:C:E$, the system using an order different from that of the searcher.) Starting from $A:B:E:C$ he will also find all narrower entry concepts, either listed immediately or indicated by cross-references.

If there are many entry concepts with more than two components, this is a very cumbersome and ineffective method. In general, if the number of entry concepts is large, cross references do not provide a convenient means for retrieving entry concepts, as anybody following the cross references in LC Subject Headings can confirm.

2.2.2 The second possibility is to establish an actual information retrieval system for entry concepts. In such a system, one would express the search question by a combination of concepts contained in a "core classification scheme" consisting of elemental or nearly elemental concepts. One would then retrieve all entry concepts (subject headings, LC class numbers, etc.) which are equal to or narrower than the search request formulation. Such a system could be peek-a-boo system (if the entry concepts are numbered serially), an edge-notched card file or a computerized system. The most likely possibility, however, would be a printed index of the combinatorial type. Foskett's rotated index is such an index. It shows every entry concept under each of its single components. The same purpose is achieved by a KWIC-index, indexing strings of terms or strings of notational symbols. More convenient, but also of much larger size, would be an index showing each entry concept under each pair of components. The SLIC index goes even further showing a compound entry concept under each combination of components. The PRECIS system could also be used for producing such an index. A chain index is another example. However, a chain index rather confuses the matter by being two things at once: an index to entry concepts in terms of their constituents as well as an alphabetical index. (We may note, parenthetically, that this remark applies to some degree to the "relative" alphabetical index to DC, and even, to a lesser degree, to the alphabetical indexes for the LC schedules.) It would be much clearer and probably also much more useful to separate these two functions and to provide a chain index in which the constituents are expressed by their notation, and an alphabetical index to the schedules.

An index constructed according to one of these methods would make the use of, for example, the LC subject headings much easier both in indexing and in searching (see Fig. 7).

Two further remarks are in order:

1. Combinatorial indexes usually are designed in such a way that it is easy to retrieve those entry concepts which are equal to the search request formulation or narrower than the search request formulation due to combination (see 2.1); that is, for the search request formulation A:B the narower entry concept A:B:C is found easily. The problem of retrieving also the narrower concept A:B', where B' is narrower than B, is not at all or not as well solved (in coordinate indexing systems this problem may be solved by generic posting, as we have seen in 2.1 and in fig. 6). The searcher has therefore to be careful while using combinatorial indexes.

2. Some of the considerations of this section apply also to combinatorial indexes used in primary information retrieval systems.

2.3 *Selection and arrangement of entry concepts*

In systems using compound entry concepts there is the problem what entry concepts to include and also the problem how to arrange the entry concepts in the file (catalog, shelves). Both problems are usually discussed under the heading "enumerative vs. synthetic schemes". In the following, we make a refined analysis of these problems. We introduce three aspects according to which classification schemes should be analyzed.

(1) The first aspect is concerned with the problem: how are the compound concepts designated? Are they designated by their own, independent symbol (possibility [1a]) or are they designated by a chain of constituent symbols, each constituent symbol presenting one of the conceptual components (possibility [1b])? Examples for possibility [1a] are the LC classification (the independent symbols being LC class numbers) and subject headings (the independent symbols being natural language terms). (We may remark that, not too seldom, subject headings consist of a string of constituent symbols, especially if standardized subheadings are used.) An example for possibility [1b] is, of course, faceted classification.

Note: It is possible to have independent symbols for the compound entry concepts and still express them by semantic factors. For possibility [1b] it is obviously necessary to express the compound entry concepts by semantic factors.

(2) Sequence of entry concepts.
We note first that once a mechanism for the retrieval of compound entry concepts as described in section 2.2 has been established, the sequence of the entry concepts is less significant. We could even number them serially as they arise. This would then be a system in the category

[1a] above (independent symbol for compound entry concepts). Usually, however, in such systems one of the following procedures is applied:
(2a1) The entry concepts are arranged according to the alphabetical sequence of the terms chosen to designate the entry concepts (this is, of course, the case of subject headings).

(2a2) The concepts are arranged according to independent notational symbols chosen to designate the concepts. The notational symbols usually lead to some kind of classified order. There is plenty of discretion and arbitrary decision-making in the arrangement. For example, if a subdivision by country is used in different places, a different sequence of countries can be chosen in each instance.

(2b1) In systems where the entry concepts are designated by strings of constituent symbols, the place of an entry concept is completely determined by the string. This ensures, for example, that at every place where a subdivision by countries is used the countries appear in the same sequence. But there may still be considerable or complete discretion as to the sequence of constituent symbols in the string ("citation order"). (See the example given in figure 1B.)

(2b2) With all the procedures for sequencing discussed up to now it is necessary to look up an entry concept in a listing in order to determine the symbol used for its designation. Provided every new entry concept is allowed in the system (see below) this is avoided in schemes that prescribe a citation order completely in every instance, such as in faceted classifications.

Notes:

(i) The designer of a system which uses independent notational symbols is free to adhere to the restrictions put forward in possibility (2b1) or (2b2) (faceted classification) in constructing his sequence of entry concepts.

(ii) The constituent symbols used in (2b1) and (2b2) may be either terms to be arranged alphabetically or notational symbols.

(3) The third aspect is the degree of ease with which new entry concepts may be introduced. Is the introduction of new entry concepts forbidden at all or are there strict procedures by which they have to be approved? What is the time needed to introduce a new entry concept? What are the criteria for approval for new entry concept? A criterion might be, for example, literary warrant, i.e. one might require that the number of entries made under the new entry concept is expected to exceed a certain number. This problem is related to the problem of multiple entry. If multiple entry is allowed then one may always use two or more less compound entry concepts to make up the delineation of the document instead of introducing a new entry concept. (Note, however, that a compound entry concept available in the system should always take precedence over a combination of less compound concepts.)

In this case one should use literary warrant and/or "search warrant" as a criterion. We shall return to this problem in the following section. If multiple entry is not allowed, such as in the LC classification and in those applications of faceted classification where a policy decision for single entry has been made, the situation is more difficult. In the case of the LC classification one must either reconcile oneself to class documents by an inappropriate class number or one has to update the schedule at very short intervals. In the case of faceted classification, the indexer is allowed to form new entry concepts as he deems necessary and a procedure has to be established to update the index to the entry concepts accordingly. Note, however, that a scheme of the LC type that allows for the inclusion of very specific entry concepts and for "immediate updating" and that provides a mechanism for the retrieval of entry concepts as described in section 2.2 is operationally equivalent to a faceted classification scheme.

2.4 A unified classification scheme for different kinds of file organization

From the perspectives developed in this paper there emerges a practical proposal for the design of a classification scheme to be used in connection with different kinds of file organization. One starts from a "core classification scheme" consisting of elemental or only moderately compound concepts. These concepts are called *Core descriptors,* and they are represented by an independent symbol, such as a notation or a term. The core classification scheme is presented as a linear arrangement with cross references. In a faceted classification, the schedules would be the core classification scheme. Starting from the core classification scheme, entry concepts are formed.

In a peek-a-boo or other post-coordinate system, only descriptors are used as entry concepts.

In a card catalog or similar systems, the descriptors themselves may be used as entry concepts, too. But further entry concepts are formed by combination of descriptors, as it becomes necessary during the development of the catalogue. In the beginning, documents dealing with A:B will be entered under both A and B. If it turns out that there are a lot of search requests for A:B or a lot of documents dealing with A:B, then A:B is introduced as an entry concept, and documents dealing with A:B are entered only there. This reduces both the number of entries and the effort necessary for searching (in searching A:B it is no longer necessary to scan *all* the cards entered under A or all the cards entered under B). A document dealing with A:B:C is entered under A:B and under C (or under B:C, if this is an entry concept). A general rule may be formulated as follows (compound concepts denoted by lower case letters): Let d be the delineation of a document. An entry for the document is made under every entry concept x with d narrower than x unless d is also narrower than entry concept y and y is narrower than x.

In a shelving system, entry concepts are formed by combination of descriptors as required by the single entry rule.

In the case of card catalogs and shelving systems, an index to the entry concepts is prepared as has been described in section 2.2. This index also tells a searcher looking, for example, for B that he should also look under A:B.

The core classification scheme together with the additional entry concepts may be called an "extended classification scheme".

A few additional remarks are in order at this point.

1. Multiple entry vs. entry under compound concepts. Take the above example of documents on A:B. In one case, they are entered under both A and B. Searcher 1, looking for A, is lucky because he has all entries together at one place in the catalog. The same is true for searcher 2, looking for B. Searcher 3, looking for A:B, however, is disadvantaged because he has to scan all entries under A (or all entries under B) to find those on A:B. If the compound entry concept A:B is created and arranged after A, searcher 1, looking for A, is still lucky. Searcher 3, looking for A:B, is now lucky, too. Searcher 2, looking for B, however, is now disadvantaged because he has to follow up a cross-reference to another place of the catalog. Giving up the advantage of having fewer entries, we could help searcher 2 by arranging the new compound entry concept at a second place as B:A and making entries for this second place, too. For searcher 3, looking for A:B, this would also be convenient, because he could now enter the file at either A or B. Speaking in terms of the model sketched in section 1, this means: the compound concept A:B is arranged under each of its broader concepts. Note that such a system provides a retrieval mechanism for compound entry concepts, as described in section 2.2, right in the file itself. If we come to more compound concepts, having more components, the size of the file increases very rapidly if one uses this procedure. One must then select some particularly useful places where to put a given compound concept among all the possible ones. This is, in essence, the purpose of the PRECIS system. For each document a delineation is prepared as a combination of descriptors, structured according to special rules. The document delineation is included into the system as an entry concept (if it was not already included before). This entry concept appears at different places in the arrangement, and an entry for the document is made under each of them, preferably giving the document number. In the application of the PRECIS system in the *British National Bibliography* (BNB), we encounter a little peculiarity which might be confusing: the index to *BNB* is an index to documents. However, the full document descriptions are listed in *BNB* by DC class numbers, and the class number is the only means to look up a document description. Therefore, in the *BNB* index, class numbers are given instead of document numbers. This

should not detract from the fact that the index is an index to documents and not an index to class numbers of the type discussed in section 2.2.

2. The entry concepts for a classified catalog using multiple entry can, of course, be formed using a faceted classification scheme. Each entry concept is then designated by a string of constituent notations. A document is indexed by as many entry concepts as necessary, the appropriate notational strings are put on the catalog card, and the card is filed at the appropriate places.

The important point in this proposal is that different institutions using the same core classification scheme could extend it in different ways, adapted to their specific needs, but still maintain compatibility between their systems. Even non-essential features of the core classification scheme (for example, the sequence of main classes or facets) could be changed without destroying compatibility on a conceptual level. (There may be some practical difficulties arising from the use of different notations in both systems. But these can easily be resolved by the application of computers.) Existing schemes, such as the LC classification scheme, could be made compatible by expressing the entry concepts in terms of the core classification scheme. A properly designed core classification scheme could thus take the role of this old dream, a universal classification. This is made possible by concentrating on the basic notions of conceptual structure and leaving aside details of arrangement and file organization on which agreement cannot be achieved and which is not even always desirable.

* * *

The approach developed in this paper has also basic implications for the design of thesauri, in particular for the design of a universal cumulative thesaurus. This subject will be dealt with in a forthcoming paper.

REFERENCES

AUSTIN, D. "Prospects for a New General Classification." *J. Librarianship,* v. 1, no. 3, 1969, p. 149-169.
   Similar in conception, but far more specific as to the kind of classification. See esp. section "Implications for the Future" for section 2.4.

CORDONNIER, G. "Metalangage pour les traductions d'intercommunications entre hommes et son adaptation dans ledomaine des machines pour recherches documentaires". *In:* Kent, A., ed. *Information Retrieval and Machine Translation,* v. 2. New York, Interscience, 1961. p. 1091-1137.
   For whole paper, esp. section 2.1.3.

FOSKETT, D. J. *Classification and Indexing in the Social Sciences.* London, Butterworth, 1963.
   p. 165 and following for section 2.2.2, rotated index.

JONKER, F. "A Descriptive Continuum: a 'Generalized' Theory of Indexing."
In: Proceedings, International Conference on Scientific Information. v. 2, 1958.
p. 1291-1311.

For section 2.1.1

LIBBEY, M. A. "The Use of Second Order Descriptors for Document Retrieval."
American Documentation, v. 18, no. 1, 1967. p. 10-20.

For section 2.1.3 (same principle, but we do not agree to the implementation
suggested in this article)

NEEDHAM, R. M. *Research on Information Retrieval, Classification and Grouping 1957-61.* Cambridge, Cambridge Language Research Unit, 1961. 177 p.

p. 11 for section 1.1, definition of hierarchical relationships (our definition is
developed from Needham's definition)

SCHEELE, M. "Thesaurus—Baustein jeder Fachdokumentation." *Nachrichten
für Dokumentation.* v. 15, no. 1, 1964. p. 1-4.

For section 2.1.3

SHARP. J. R. "The SLIC Index." *American Documentation,* v. 17, no. 1, 1966,
p. 41-44.

For section 2.2.2

SOERGEL, D. "Mathematical Analysis of Documentation Systems; an Attempt
to a Theory of Classification and Search Request Formulation." *In: Information
Storage and Retrieval,* v. 3, no. 3, 1967, p. 129-73.

For section 1

SOERGEL, D. *Outlines of an Algorithm for the Analysis and Comparison of
Classification Systems.* Freiburg i. Br., Selbstverlag, 1965.

App. 2, section A(1) for section 1.1.3.

DISCUSSION

M. *de Grolier* disagreed with Soergel on a number of points: firstly, he
felt that the distinction between conceptual structure and file organization was not a meaningful distinction. Secondly, he believed that there
could be semantic factors for a term like "gross national product": the
only irreducible concepts, philosophically speaking, are 'being' and 'non-
being'. Thirdly, he did not agree that new entry concepts could be freely
introduced into a faceted classification. Finally, he disagreed with Soergel
when he said that dropping a restriction was a special case of weakening
a restriction, suspecting that the reverse was really true.

Mr. *Soergel* said that in the case of "gross national product" he had
probably chosen a bad example, but that the main point, i.e. the fact
that semantic factoring is based not upon language but upon concepts,
was made clear by the "White House" example. On faceted classification, he had intended to make the point that one may form any combinations of foci from different facets and then use these combinations
as entry concepts. Finally, he simply disagreed with M. de Grolier on
his last point.

Mr. *Shumway* raised the problem of conflict between the logic of the
classification maker and the logic of the users of the system.

Mr. *Soergel* replied that one must attempt to incorporate different views into the system: Wilson's example of "radar observation of bird migration" was a good one in this respect. Such a subject could belong, quite validly, to at least three broader heads: so far as conceptual structure was concerned, this could be indicated in the indexing language without difficulty, but represented considerable problems in file organization for linear searching. This example also illustrates the validity of the division into conceptual structure and file organization to which Mr. de Grolier had referred.

THE WORK OF THE BRITISH CLASSIFICATION RESEARCH GROUP

T. D. Wilson

School of Library and Information Services
*University of Maryland**

Outlines the work of the CRG paying particular attention to the period since 1962. The intention is to emphasize theoretical concerns and their impact and also to provide background information for the papers by Austin and Aitchison.

The word "classification" is one which, in relation to information retrieval, seems to evoke a curious range of responses from wholesale acceptance of the validity of the idea that the two concepts are compatible, to utter incomprehension. This, it seems, is due to the fact that "classification" evokes at least three images:

(a) that of a system for arranging books on shelves. Traditionally this is the aspect of classification which has been emphasized in the U.S.A. and which is still considered by many to be its only function;

(b) that of a basis for the subject analysis of documents, i.e. the exact specification of the subject content of documents within the framework of a classification system. This aspect has been strongly emphasized in Europe since the development of the Universal Decimal Classification scheme. In the U.S.A. this function has been performed through the use of alphabetic subject heading lists and, more recently, through the development of "thesauri";

(c) that of an aid to information retrieval, either through searching classified files prepared on the basis of (b) above, or through the provision of "classificatory maps" to alphabetically ordered manual files, or machine files ordered in a variety of ways.

In the past, attempts have been made to construct general classification systems which are capable of serving all three of the above functions. However, it is now being realized, particularly since the advent of com-

---

*Permanent address: Dept. of Librarianship, Newcastle upon Tyne Polytechnic, Newcastle upon Tyne, England.

puterized systems, that the ideal of a multi-purpose universal system is a chimera. There are good reasons for suggesting that differing functions demand differing systems, for example:

firstly: the qualities that librarians demand of shelf order systems are incompatible with the qualities demanded of systems for information retrieval. The former are expected to be comparatively stable with a brief notational system. Librarians are conservatives—change is abhorrent, especially when it costs money, and the demand for brief notation is desirable for the practical reasons of ease of ordering and ease of searching. These qualities are quite at variance with the chief requirement of systems for information retrieval which is specificity, the ability to uniquely identify the specific subject content of a document. This militates against brief notation. A second quality required of systems for information retrieval is that they must change with developments in the conceptual structure of the subject field: the more rapidly the developments are taking place the less likely is the system to be stable;

secondly: it is now theoretically feasible to create interactive computer systems which respond to the searcher's own conceptual system. It has been suggested that this removes the necessity for any classificatory structure. However, while for some types of searches natural language matches may provide sufficient information to satisfy the user, it seems highly probable that for applications where very high recall is required there must be some structure either in the machine or available to the user to assist him in the development of his search strategy. Such a classificatory structure must be capable of continuous development and reorganization on the basis of the conceptual analysis of the documents and search requests received.

The alternative types of classification scheme which are available are: (a) universe of knowledge systems, which may also be called subject specification systems, and (b) universe of concepts systems, or concept identification systems. The distinction may be expressed briefly as follows: the first type of system assumes a finite universe of knowledge which can be subdivided until the individual concept is reached—the chain of classes then represents a subject, e.g.

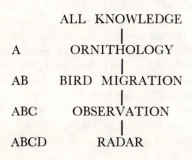

ABCD is now the class number which will serve quite adequately to identify the location of a book entitled *Radar Observation of Bird Migration*. Note, however, that "radar" may have a totally different piece of notation elsewhere in the same system, e.g.

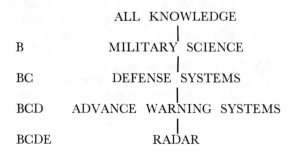

ALL KNOWLEDGE

B   MILITARY SCIENCE

BC   DEFENSE SYSTEMS

BCD   ADVANCE WARNING SYSTEMS

BCDE   RADAR

Furthermore, another classification system may produce this different but equally valid subdivision of the universe:

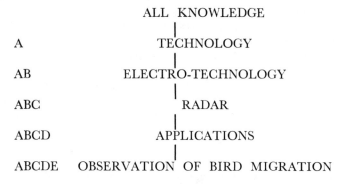

ALL KNOWLEDGE

A   TECHNOLOGY

AB   ELECTRO-TECHNOLOGY

ABC   RADAR

ABCD   APPLICATIONS

ABCDE   OBSERVATION OF BIRD MIGRATION

The universe of concepts approach is totally different: it assumes no finite universe of subjects, but approaches the problem from the point of view of grouping elemental concepts into categories, e.g. in our subject BIRD is a concept within the category "naturally occurring entities", MIGRATION is an "action", OBSERVATION is an "action", RADAR is an "artificial entity". The concepts are then uniquely identified by a notation which stands for all occurrences of the concept in subjects. Thus, if RADAR is represented in its category by the notation ABCD, that notational string will always represent RADAR regardless of the subject in which it appears. The same will be done for all other concepts. This has two significant consequences: (a) such a system is ideal for machine retrieval and (b) such a system is totally useless for shelf ordering because of the cumbersome notational strings. Therefore if the machine information retrieval system is used for the subject analysis of documents in an information center in which browsing by users is a customary and allowed mode of operation, two systems are necessary.

The work of the Classification Research Group (CRG), particularly over the last 10 years, can be viewed in terms of the gradual realization of the concepts described above, though, as members of the CRG readily testify, there is at present no uniformity of thought within the Group about one kind of system versus the other.

The CRG is a curious body: D.J. Foskett, in his report on the first ten years of its work, characterized it as:

> ". . . a typically British affair, with no resources beyond the native wit of its members, no allegiance to any existing system of classification, no fixed target, no recognition by the British Government (naturally) and at first only an amused tolerance from the library profession." (1)

In its early years the CRG's activities were concentrated predominantly in three areas:

(a) The development of special classification schemes for a wide range of subject areas from Soil Science (2) to Music (3) on the basis of Ranganathan's "facet analysis". In the course of this work the members of the group moved away from Ranganathan's concept of five "fundamental categories" (Personality, Matter, Energy, Space and Time) toward a set of categories of more pragmatic nature with, nevertheless, a wide range of applicability, i.e. thing, kind, part, material, property, process, operation, agent, space, and time. This kind of approach was also employed by another member of the group, E.J. Coates, in his work on alphabetical subject indexing (4) which he was able to develop in the *British Technology Index*.

(b) The investigation of notational systems for classification schemes. In this area a major conclusion was that a notation could be purely ordinal, i.e. that it need not express the hierarchical structure of the classification scheme. Such an idea was, of course, implicit in Bliss' demand for a brief notation and was applied to a certain extent in his own scheme, but the idea was logically developed by the CRG to the extent of proposing, and in some special schemes using, a purely ordinal notation. A development of this idea led to the invention by Coates of "retroactive ordinal notation".

> "The brilliantly simple idea that if each facet were allotted part of the alphabet and no subdivision began with a letter earlier in the alphabet than the letter which began the facet, early parts of the alphabet could be used to subdivide later; thus the same notational symbols could, without confusion, show both subdivisions of one facet and the relations of one facet to another" (1)

e.g. in the *British Catalogue of Music Classification* F = Female voices, EN = Accompanied by chamber orchestra and DGH = Masses, thus

FENDGH

represents "Masses for female voices accompanied by chamber orchestra".

(c) The analysis of relationships between concepts. In the early years one member in particular, namely J.E.L. Farradane, chose this as his research area and evolved his now well known "relational operators". (5) These relators were based upon a theory in the psychology of thinking and, interestingly, they could also be used as the basis for facet analysis although Farradane's original intent was that they should be used for linking natural language terms in an alphabetical system.

To conclude this review of the early work of the CRG it is probably not too far from the truth to say that most of the Group's activity was concentrated upon the development of specialized systems for relatively narrow fields of knowledge but that this was always done with a view to the discovery of general principles and fruitful lines of investigation.

In 1962 the NATO Science Foundation awarded the Library Association a grant of $14,000 to study the feasibility of a new general classification scheme and the L.A. appointed the CRG as its agent in this research. Since that time the group's activities have been directed to an examination of the problems of general, as distinct from special, classification schemes although no further funds have been forthcoming for this work.

The CRG's work in relation to the NATO grant and subsequently has been concentrated in three areas:

Firstly, the determination of principles for the categorization of concepts. The first research worker under the NATO grant was Helen Tomlinson who revised the set of categories mentioned earlier, the revised list being:

 Entities
  naturally occurring
  artefacts
  mentefacts (i.e. theories and other systems of ideas)
 Parts
 Constituents
 Properties
 Self activities
 Relations at own levels
 Relations at other levels
 Method of study

Mrs. Tomlinson prepared a number of outline schemes for various subject fields based on this set of categories or variations thereon, e.g. that for Physics used the categories:

> Concrete entities
> Properties of entities
> Activities
> Properties of activities

an analysis which foreshadowed the list developed by Tomlinson's successor on the project, Derek Austin:

> Entities
>> Concrete
>>> Naturally occurring
>>> Artificial
>> Abstract (mentefacts)
> Attributes
>> Activities
>> Properties

Work on categorization continues, Austin having stated recently that he favours a simplification of the list to read:

> Independent entities
> Dependent entities
>> Actions

The second area of investigation relates to the ordering of concepts within categories. In this field the Group's interests centered on the possibility of using the 'theory of integrative levels' (8). Since the CRG's work at this time was related to research into a general classification scheme the basic notion was that the entities category could be organized according to this theory into the following "classes":

> Physical entities
> Chemical entities
> Heterogeneous non-living entities
> Artefacts
> Biological entities
> Man
> Mentefacts

For specialized areas Tomlinson linked integrative levels and categories in tables which analyzed concepts in the field, e.g. in Physics:

Concrete entities	Properties of entities	Activities
Fundamental particle Electron Photon — — — — — — charge Neutrino etc. Atom	 atomic weight	Motion flow streaming emission scattering attraction conduction etc.

As a result of this activity, including a careful analysis of integrative level theory by Austin, (9) the group reached two main conclusions:

firstly: integrative levels formed a branching structure rather than a single sequence, thus: (10)

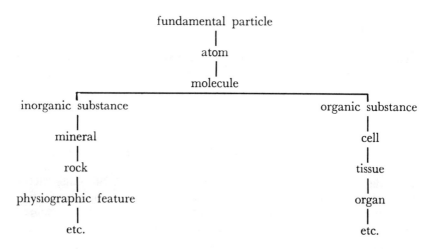

The implication of this was, of course, that the theory could not offer a basis for an unequivocal single sequence of classes;

secondly: the theory was of little use for determining an order for abstract ideas (mentefacts) or artefacts.

At this point Austin proceeded to search for further principles which could be used to augment integrative level theory. He suggested the principles of consecutiveness and causal dependence and noted that this leads to an initial division of entities into naturally occurring entities, arranged into a causal or time-dependent series, and artificial entities, which, according to the principle of consecutiveness, are placed later in the sequence than the organisms responsible for their creation. Furthermore, causal dependence suggests that one artificial thing is most usefully related to another in terms of function or purpose. This latter principle requires the establishment of a series of needs or "drives"—the sociologist's "fundamental prerequisites" may be of help here. The same principle may also provide a basis for ordering mentefacts.

The third area of investigation was that of relationships between concepts: as noted above, one member of the group, J. Farradane, had been particularly interested in this aspect of classification research and had produced his own set of relational operators. Austin, however, in beginning his work in this area chose to take a more pragmatic view than that of Farradane and produced a rather more intelligible set of role indicators,* which he discusses in his paper to this Symposium.

The CRG's conclusions on this area of general classification schemes were: firstly, that certain principles had been discovered which gave hope that a satisfactory solution to the problems of such schemes could be found; secondly, that a possible and testable approach would be to construct two classified thesauri — one of entities, the other of attributes — organized according to the above mentioned principles. Classifying would then consist of selecting terms from the thesauri and linking their notational elements using the set of roles developed by Austin. To date no funds have been forthcoming for this work to be carried out, although a grant has been made available for work on PRECIS (Preserved Context Indexing System), the alphabetical indexing system developed by Austin for use in the *British National Bibliography* as a result of his work on the NATO project.

In order to dispel the impression that the CRG's work has been solely related to the problems of general classification schemes it is necessary to draw attention to some other activities. Members of the Group have continued to produce special faceted classification schemes. One of these, the Library Science Classification Scheme is currently used by *Library and Information Science Abstracts (LISA)* as well as in two or three library school libraries. The scheme is currently undergoing revision and some discussion is taking place over the citation order of facets: originally the scheme had Kind of Library as its primary facet, but some dissatisfaction has been voiced about this and the suggestion has been made that Operation should be the primary facet. So far as the major body of users of *LISA* is concerned, this is probably true.

Another scheme is the subject of a paper in this Symposium, i.e. the English Electric *Thesaurofacet*. Mrs. Aitchison, who was responsible for

---

*As Soergel has pointed out (11) the use of role indicators in a concept string is logically equivalent to the use of relators, i.e., (Role 1) TERM A (Role 2) TERM B = TERM A (Relator X) TERM B

the earlier faceted classification scheme for the same company has noted that the decision was made to reverse the earlier decision to dispense with 'main classes' in the system and this, interestingly, bears some relationship to D.W. Langridge's concern that the CRG has given little thought to 'disciplines' in its study of the principles of a general classification scheme. The most interesting aspect of the *Thesaurofacet*, however, is its attempt to marry a faceted classification scheme to a thesaurus which also serves as the alphabetic subject index. One thereby achieves the hierarchical display of terms which is desirable for showing relationships together with the expression in the thesaurus of those relationships which a single hierarchical sequence cannot express. This illustrates that members of the Group who employ faceted or categorical classification techniques are willing to accept alternative methods of displaying indexing languages while retaining those techniques as the base upon which to build.

To conclude this discussion of CRG activity, a project which has interested a number of the members of the Group is that concerning the 'intermediate lexicon' i.e.:

> ". . . a tool or piece of software whereby the indexing terms or notation which have been applied to a given document entry under one indexing system may be converted to their conceptional equivalents in any other indexing system by clerical means . . . The conversion could employ the method of indirect concordance between systems, i.e. there will exist a concordance of equivalence between each of the indexing systems of the Intermediate Lexicon (12)"

A project, financed in Great Britain by the Office for Scientific and Technical Information, is now underway to test the feasibility of this idea. This test will involve, as a first approximation of the functions of the intermediate lexicon, the translation of the concepts in the CRG library science classification scheme into German with the assistance of a group in Frankfurt. Dr. David Weeks of the American University is also participating from the interesting point of view of the need for translation into "American English". Subsequently, tests will be run on the production of index entries in German automatically from the English language indexing of documents. These will then be examined to discover whether or not the index entries in German are meaningful and a further check will seek to discover whether the reverse process also works satisfactorily.

It would be wrong to conclude a paper such as this without saying something about the impact of the Group's activity, which has been considerable. In Britain, the Group has had a tremendous impact upon the teaching of classification and information retrieval both as a result of the activities of those members of the Group who are teachers and as a result of the many writings produced by other members.

Secondly, the special systems produced by members of the Group have been applied to a wide variety of organizations, some of which are of national significance, e.g. the *British Catalogue of Music* scheme, the *British Technology Index* indexing system, and the library science scheme used by *Library and Information Science Abstracts.*

Finally, over the years the *British National Bibliography* has pioneered the use of advances in classification and indexing theory in its use of faceted techniques for expanding parts of the *Decimal Classification Scheme* not sufficiently detailed for its requirements, in its use of chain indexing techniques developed by Ranganathan, and, most recently, in its adoption of Austin's PRECIS for the subject index to BNB.

Although the Group has been very active since 1952 it would be wrong to suppose that their work is finished: there is still much to be done in relation to the problem of ordering entities other than those which are naturally-occurring; a pilot test of the kind of classification system proposed by Austin is needed; and finally there is much fundamental work which needs to be done on the relation between concept formation and classification and indexing. This list by no means exhausts the possibilities, so we may expect the CRG to flourish for a number of years to come.

REFERENCES

1. FOSKETT, D.J. "The Classification Research Group 1952-1962." *Libri,* v. 12, no. 2, 1962, p. 127-138.

2. VICKERY, B.C. *Classification and Indexing in Science.* 2nd ed. London, Butterworths, 1959. Appendix B. p. 195-203.

3. COATES, E.J. *The British Catalogue of Music Classification.* London, Library Association, 1960.

4. COATES, E.J. *Subject Catalogues: Headings and Structure.* London, Library Association, 1960.

5. FARRADANE, J. "Relational indexing." *Indexer,* v. 2, no. 4, 1961, p. 127-133.

6. AUSTIN, D. "Prospects for a New General Classification." *Journal of Librarianship,* v. 1, no. 3, 1969, p. 149-169.

7. FEIBLEMAN, J.K. "Integrative Levels in Nature," *in:* KYLE, B. ed. *Focus on Information and Communication.* London, Aslib, 1968, p. 27-41.

8. FOSKETT, D.J. *Classification for a General Index Language.* London, Library Association, 1970.

9. LIBRARY ASSOCIATION. *Classification and Information Control: Papers Representing the World of the Classification Research Group from 1960 to 1968.* London, Library Association, 1970.

10. FOSKETT, D.J. op. cit., ref. 8.

11. SOERGEL, D. "Mathematical Analysis of Documentation Systems." *Information Storage and Retrieval,* v. 3, no. 3, 1967, p. 129-173.

12. CLASSIFICATION RESEARCH GROUP. Bulletin no. 9. *Journal of Documentation,* v. 24, no. 4, 1968, p. 273-298.

THESAUROFACET
A New Concept in Subject Retrieval Schemes

JEAN AITCHISON

Consultant in Information and Library Systems
17, Ravenbank Road, Luton, Bedfordshire

The English Electric *Thesaurofacet* is a combined faceted classification and thesaurus, for engineering and related subjects. In perspective, it is seen not so much as a departure from existing practice in thesaurus construction; but the culmination of a trend towards the integration of complementary alphabetical and systematic sequences. However, it can claim to be a new concept in subject retrieval, since it is the first indexing language designed for use in both pre-coordination and post-coordinate situations. The structure of *Thesaurofacet* is examined. Each term appears both in the thesaurus and in the schedules. In the schedules the term is displayed in the most appropriate facet and hierarchy: the thesaurus supplements this information by indicating alternate hierarchies and other relationships that cut across the classified arrangement. The thesaurus also controls word forms and synonyms and acts as an alphabetical index to the class numbers. The part played by classification during compilation of *Thesaurofacet* is discussed and some consideration given to the problems of updating, including the use of synthesis for building new concepts. Finally, methods of application of *Thesaurofacet* are analysed for post-coordinate and pre-coordinate information retrieval systems.

Thesaurofacet in perspective

Thesaurofacet (1), the successor to the English Electric *Faceted Classification for Engineering* (2), integrates a faceted classification system with a thesaurus. At the time of compilation, it was thought to be an entirely new species of retrieval language; but it is now realised that Thesaurofacet is not so much a new concept in subject retrieval systems, as a refinement of techniques in thesaurus construction, which have been evolving since the mid-sixties.

To put *Thesaurofacet* into perspective, it is necessary to study the development of classification techniques in thesaurus construction. The thesauri of the late fifties and early sixties were structured purely alphabetically. The limitations of the alphabetical arrangement led to the employment of classification aids, ranging from the broad to the detailed, and from auxiliary to integrated devices. Fig. 1 is a list of the categories of classification aids which may be employed, with examples from specific thesauri.

Fig. 1. CLASSIFICATORY AIDS IN THESAURI

	Broad Subject Groups	Clusters (manual)	Clusters (statistical)	Arrow-graphs	Semantic factoring	Hierarchical displays of BT/NTs	Full hierarchical classifications	Fundamental facets only	Full faceted classification	Classification used in compilation	Classification not used in compilation	Notation used for shelf arrangement
Term lists												
Lloyds					X							
Shell		X								X		
Hutton & Rostron		X			X					X		
Lesk			X							X		
Structured Thesauri												
TEST	X					X					X	
NASA	X					X					X	
EURATOM				X							X	
IRRD				X							X	
MeSH							X			X		
McClelland								X		X		
Gertrude London										X		
Bauer								X		X		
Dym								X		X		
Marlot & Moureau								X		X		
CIRIA									X	X		
Croghan									X	X		X
Thesaurofacet									X	X		X

The re-arrangement of the thesaurus terms under a fairly broad classification scheme is the simplest classification device and is illustrated in the *TEST Thesaurus* (3) (fig. 2) and also in the NASA and other thesauri. A second device is the clustering, or clumping, of related terms. This technique can be used as a tool in thesaurus construction, as in the Hutton and Rostron Thesaurus (4) or as an aid to the visual display of the alphabetical arrangement of terms, in the form of "semantic maps", "arrowgraphs" or "terminological charts", as used in the IRRD Thesaurus (5) and in the Euratom and INIS thesauri (6, 7) (fig. 3). The mechanised clustering of terms is still very much at the experimental stage (8, 9) and as yet it is complementing, rather than replacing, manual techniques.

Another group of classification aids is concerned with purely hierarchical relationships. The traditional thesaurus method of indicating broader and narrower term hierarchies has proved unsatisfactory because not all levels of hierarchy can be displayed alphabetically at once, or if the terms are arranged alphabetically, it is not possible to distinguish between different hierarchical levels. To overcome this disadvantage, mechanised thesauri, such as TEST, NASA, BNB, and INSPEC can produce automatically hierarchical trees, arranged with the broadest concept at the head of the display (See fig. 4). The CDA Thesaurus (10) displays terms in generic trees (see fig. 5) whilst the MeSH Thesaurus provides in its "Tree structures" (11), a detailed hierarchical classification of the terms in the alphabetical MeSH. This replaces altogether, rather than supplements, the traditional display of genus/species (BT/NT) entries in the main thesaurus. Terms may appear in several hierarchies, as for example, "tinea pedis" (athlete's foot) which appears in four hierarchies (see fig. 6).

Finally, facet analysis can be used as a classification device in thesaurus construction. Fundamental facet groups have been used for some time now as a tool in the process of thesaurus compilation. Eleanor Dym (12) used them in the production of a thesaurus for paint terminology (see fig. 7). The field was divided according to a "road map" into "materials", "equipment", "supplies", "process and method" and "property characteristic or condition". Similarly Mulvihill (13) employed fundamental facet groupings against which to organise terms in the petroleum industry. In Europe, facet techniques have been used by Bauer (14, 15) in chemical thesaurus construction, and by Marlot and Moureau (16) for a petroleum industry thesaurus.

From the use of broad facet groups in thesaurus construction, it was a small step to the use of a fully faceted classification with a thesaurus. *Thesaurofacet,* which integrates a detailed, as opposed to an outline, facet classification with an alphabetical thesaurus, was probably an inevitable development. Since its publication, there have been two further

FIG. 2. BROAD GROUPS (TEST)

Subject Category Fields and Groups

01 Aeronautics
*01 01
01 02 Aeronautics
01 03 Aircraft
01 04 Aircraft flight instrumentation
01 05 Air facilities

02 Agriculture
02 01 Agricultural chemistry
02 02 Agricultural economics
02 03 Agricultural engineering
02 04 Agronomy and horticulture
02 05 Animal husbandry
02 06 Forestry

03 Astronomy and astrophysics
03 01 Astronomy
03 02 Astrophysics
03 03 Celestial mechanics

04 Atmospheric sciences
04 01 Atmospheric physics
04 02 Meteorology

05 Behavioral and social sciences
05 01 Administration and
management
*05 02 Information sciences
05 03 Economics
05 04 History, law, and
political science
05 05 Human factors engineering
05 06 Humanities
05 07 Linguistics
*05 08
05 09 Personnel selection, training,
and evaluation
*05 10 Psychology
05 11 Sociology

06 Biological and medical sciences
06 01 Biochemistry
06 02 Bioengineering
06 03 Biology
06 04 Bionics
06 05 Clinical medicine
06 06 Environmental biology
06 07 Escape, rescue, and survival
06 08 Food
06 09 Hygiene and sanitation
*06 10
06 11 Life support
*06 12 Medical equipment and
supplies
06 13 Microbiology
06 14 Personnel selection and
maintenance (medical)
06 15 Pharmacology
06 16 Physiology

06 17 Protective equipment
06 18 Radiobiology
06 19 Stress physiology
06 20 Toxicology
06 21 Weapon effects

07 Chemistry
07 01 Chemical engineering
07 02 Inorganic chemistry
07 03 Organic chemistry
*07 04 Physical and general
chemistry
07 05 Radio and radiation
chemistry

08 Earth sciences and oceanography
08 01 Biological oceanography
08 02 Cartography
08 03 Dynamic oceanography
08 04 Geochemistry
08 05 Geodesy
08 06 Geography
08 07 Geology and mineralogy
08 08 Hydrology and limnology
08 09 Mining engineering
08 10 Physical oceanography
08 11 Seismology
08 12 Snow, ice and permafrost
08 13 Soil mechanics
*08 14 Geomagnetism

09 Electronics and electrical engineering
09 01 Components
09 02 Computers
09 03 Electronic and electrical
engineering
09 04 Information theory
09 05 Subsystems
09 06 Telemetry

*10 Nonpropulsive energy conversion
10 01 Conversion techniques
10 02 Power sources
10 03 Energy storage

11 Materials
11 01 Adhesives and seals
11 02 Ceramics, refractories,
and glasses
11 03 Coatings, colorants, and
finishes
11 04 Composite materials
11 05 Fibers and textiles
*11 06 Metals
11 07 Miscellaneous materials
11 08 Oils, lubricants, and
hydraulic fluids
11 09 Plastics

FIG. 3. CLUSTERS - ARROWGRAPHS (INIS)

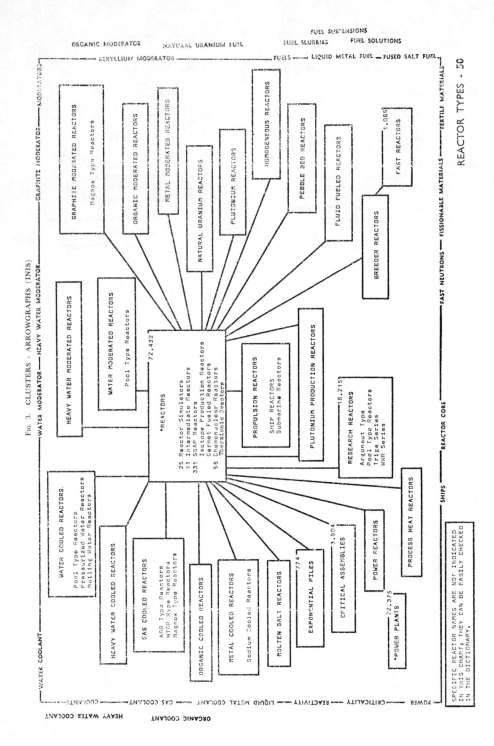

REACTOR TYPES - 50

SPECIFIC REACTOR NAMES ARE NOT INDICATED
IN THIS CHART, THEY CAN BE EASILY CHECKED
IN THE DICTIONARY.

Fɪɢ. 4. HIERARCHICAL DISPLAYS (TEST)

Detectors

. Acoustic detectors
. . Hydrophones
. . Sonobuoys
. Airborne detectors
. Depth detectors
. Fuze target detectors
. Gas detectors
. Ground based detectors
. Infrared quantum detectors
. . Infrared quantum detectors
. . . Infrared photoconductors
. . . Infrared photovoltaic detectors
. . Infrared thermal detectors
. . . Infrared bolometers
. . . . Infrared thermistors
. Leak detectors
. Ordnance detectors
. . Ground fire locators
. . Mine detectors
. . . Acoustic mine detectors
. . . Magnetic mine detectors
. . Mortar locator radar
. Pressure sensors
. Shipborne detectors
. Spaceborne detectors
. . Micrometeoroid detectors
. Sun sensors
. Swimmer detection devices
. Ultraviolet detectors

FIG. 5. GENERIC TREES (CDA)

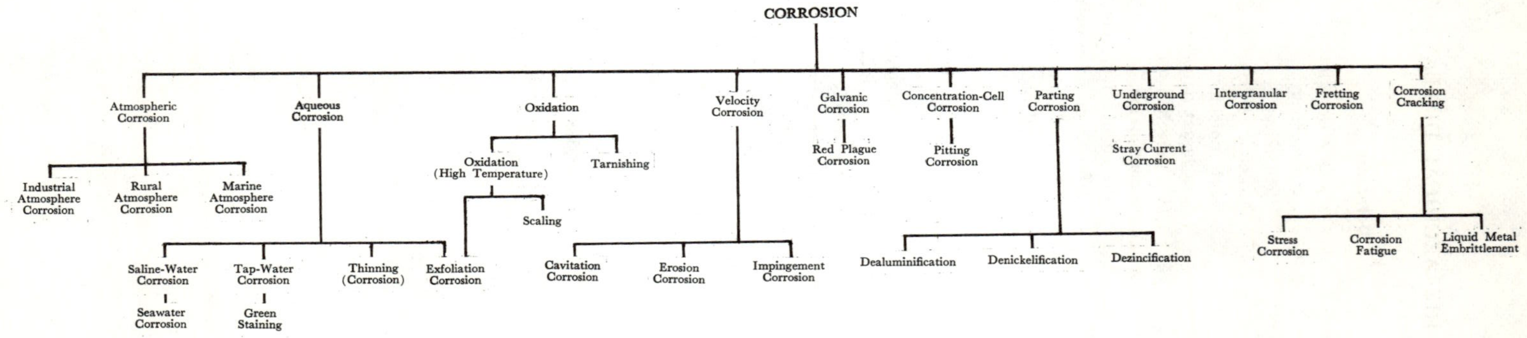

Fig. 6. GENERIC TREES (MeSH)

THESAURUS

TINEA FAVOSA
C1.40.27.1; C12.14.55.1
X FAVUS (C1, C12)

▶ **TINEA PEDIS**
C1.40.27.1; C12.14.55.1
C12.31.32; C17.25.24.1
X ATHLETE'S FOOT (C1, C12, C17)

TINEA UNGUIUM
C1.40.27.1; C12.14.55.1
X ONYCHOMYCOSIS (C1, C12)

TINEA VERSICOLOR
C1.40.27.1; C12.14.55.1
X PITYRIASIS VERSICOLOR (C1, C12)

TINNITUS
C11.65.50;

TIOCARLID see THIOCARLIDE (D3)

TISSUE ADHESIVES
D13.99; E4.124.

TREE STRUCTURES

C12 - SKIN DISEASES

DERMATOMYCOSIS	C12.14.	C1.40.27.	C12.94.8.	
ACTINOMYCOSIS, CERVICOFACIAL	C12.14.11.	C1.10.16.1		
CHROMOBLASTOMYCOSIS	C12.14.16.	C1.40.27.1		
MADUROMYCOSIS	C12.14.33.	C1.10.48.1	C1.40.27.1	
MONILIASIS, CUTANEOUS	C12.14.44.	C1.40.27.1	C1.40.45.1	
TINEA	C12.14.55.	C1.40.27.1		
TINEA CAPITIS	C12.14.55.1	C1.40.27.1	C12.76.23.	
TINEA FAVOSA	C12.14.55.1	C1.40.27.1		
▶ TINEA PEDIS	C12.14.55.1	C1.40.27.1	C12.31.32.	C17.25.24.1
TINEA UNGUIUM	C12.14.55.1	C1.40.27.1		
TINEA VERSICOLOR	C12.14.55.1		C1.40.27.1	
DERMATOMYOSITIS	C12.16.	C3.80.35.1	C17.16.18.	
ERYTHEMA	C12.19.			
ERYTHEMA NODOSUM	C12.21.			
ERYTHRODERMA	C12.24.			
EXANTHEMA	C12.26.	C1.30.23.		
EXANTHEMA SUBITUM	C12.26.21.	C1.100.21.		
WISSLER'S SYNDROME	C12.26.43.	C3.10.56.1	C3.90.54.1	C14.22.36.1
FACIAL DERMATOSES	C12.29.			
ACNE	C12.29.21.	C12.86.39.1		
ROSACEA	C12.29.43.			
FAVRE-RACOUCHOT SYNDROME	C12.30.			
FOOT DERMATOSES	C12.31.	C17.25.24.1		
▶ TINEA PEDIS	C12.31.32.	C1.40.27.1	C12.14.55.1	C17.25.24.1
HAND DERMATOSES	C12.34.			
ICHTHYOSIS	C12.36.	C16.70.35.		

Fig. 7. FUNDAMENTAL FACETS (Dym)

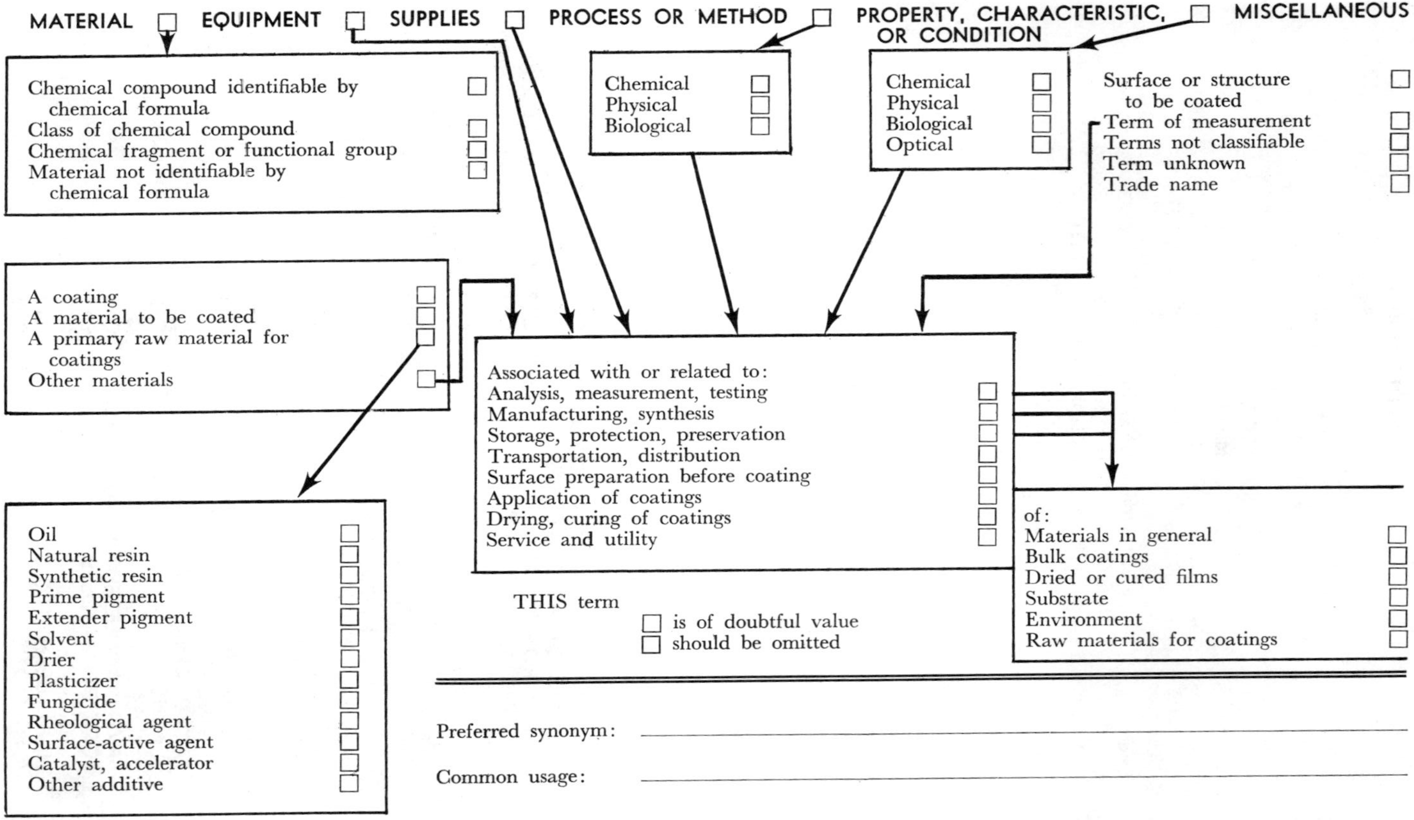

MATERIAL □ EQUIPMENT □ SUPPLIES □ PROCESS OR METHOD □ PROPERTY, CHARACTERISTIC, OR CONDITION □ MISCELLANEOUS

Chemical compound identifiable by chemical formula
Class of chemical compound
Chemical fragment or functional group
Material not identifiable by chemical formula

PROCESS OR METHOD
Chemical
Physical
Biological

PROPERTY, CHARACTERISTIC, OR CONDITION
Chemical
Physical
Biological
Optical

MISCELLANEOUS
Surface or structure to be coated
Term of measurement
Terms not classifiable
Term unknown
Trade name

A coating
A material to be coated
A primary raw material for coatings
Other materials

Associated with or related to:
Analysis, measurement, testing
Manufacturing, synthesis
Storage, protection, preservation
Transportation, distribution
Surface preparation before coating
Application of coatings
Drying, curing of coatings
Service and utility

of:
Materials in general
Bulk coatings
Dried or cured films
Substrate
Environment
Raw materials for coatings

Oil
Natural resin
Synthetic resin
Prime pigment
Extender pigment
Solvent
Drier
Plasticizer
Fungicide
Rheological agent
Surface-active agent
Catalyst, accelerator
Other additive

THIS term □ is of doubtful value □ should be omitted

Preferred synonym: _____

Common usage: _____

Fig. 8. FULL-FACET CLASSIFICATION (CIRIA)

THESAURUS

Flocculants	H5357
UF Coagulants	
Gelling agents	
Flocculating	G4023
Floodlighting	J6125
Flood protection equipment	F2131
Flooded system evaporators	J4039
Floor layers	
USE Floorers	F0411
Floorers	F0411
UF Floor layers	
Flooring	J2111
Flooring tiles	J0827
UF Paving tiles	
▶ Floors	J9105

SCHEDULES

J9098	False ceilings
▶ J9105	**Floors**

    Note Terminology relating to floors has been brought to this point for convenience. Floors which serve a structural function should be indexed as Structure/Floors in indexing systems using compound headings.

J9112	Non self centering floors	(Floors special to concrete)
▶ J9119	Self centering floors	"
J9126	Plank floors	"
J9133	Partially self centering floors	"
J9140	One direction spanning slab floors	
J1947	Two direction spanning slab floors	
J9151	Suspended floors	(Floors by suspended/not suspended)
J9158	Solid floors i.e. supported	"
	other than at the ends	
J9165	Beam and covering floors	(Floors by construction)
J9172	Joists and covering floors	
J9179	Joist plus infill floors	"
J9186	Joist and filler block floors	
J9193	Slab floors	"
▶ J9200	Flush slab floors	
J9207	Plank floors *J9126	
J9214	Beam plus slab floors	"
J9221	Beam and slab floors	

tools produced on similar lines. These are the Construction Industry Research and Information Association's (CIRIA) *Thesaurus for the construction industry* (17) and Croghan's *Thesaurus for non-book materials* (18). The notation used by the CIRIA Thesaurus (see fig. 8) is not suitable for shelf arrangement and filing of documents, although Croghan's work (see fig. 9), like *Thesaurofacet* may be used as a multipurpose tool for conventional classified catalogues and shelf ordering as well as for coordinate indexing and computer applications.

FIG. 9. FULL-FACET CLASSIFICATION (Croghan)

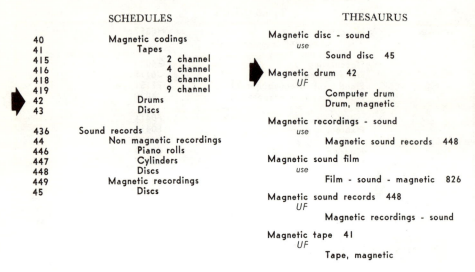

SCHEDULES

40	Magnetic codings	
41	Tapes	
415		2 channel
416		4 channel
418		8 channel
419		9 channel
42	Drums	
43	Discs	
436	Sound records	
44	Non magnetic recordings	
446	Piano rolls	
447	Cylinders	
448	Discs	
449	Magnetic recordings	
45	Discs	

THESAURUS

Magnetic disc - sound
   use
      Sound disc 45

Magnetic drum 42
   UF
      Computer drum
      Drum, magnetic

Magnetic recordings - sound
   use
      Magnetic sound records 448

Magnetic sound film
   use
      Film - sound - magnetic 826

Magnetic sound records 448
   UF
      Magnetic recordings - sound

Magnetic tape 41
   UF
      Tape, magnetic

Structure of Thesaurofacet

The *Thesaurofacet* consists of two sections: the classification schedules and the alphabetical thesaurus. The terms appear twice, once in the thesaurus and once in the schedules, the link between the two locations being the notation or class number. At each location, different information is given about the term. The two parts of the system are complementary; if consulted apart, they are incomplete. If the user has a specific term in mind, he may enter the thesaurus at that term. If, for example, the term is "Television camera tubes" (see fig. 10 (a) i), he will be directed, via the class number MCE to the schedule, "Electron tubes" (see fig. 10 (a) ii). Here, a visual display shows the hierarchy in which the term primarily belongs. Its immediate genus is "Cathode ray tubes" and above this there are the broader generic terms "Electron beam deflection tubes" and "Electron tubes", while the narrower term is "Television colour camera tubes". There are also related terms which are species of the common genus "Cathode ray tubes": these include "Image converter tubes" and "Television picture tubes". The classification entry can display these relationships more effectively than a conventional thesaurus entry (see fig. 10 (b)), especially in the case of the broader terms, where the alphabetical arrangement does not distinguish between the three generic levels.

After consulting the classification schedule, the user should return to the thesaurus for additional information about the terms. In the case of "Television camera tubes" (fig. 10 (i)), the thesaurus entry shows

FIGURE 10(a). THE COMPLEMENTARY PARTS OF THE THESAUROFACET

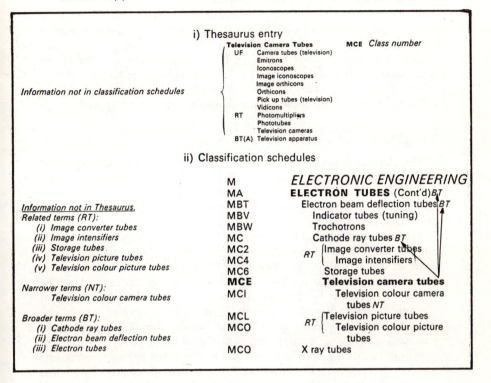

FIGURE 10(b). CONVENTIONAL THESAURUS ENTRY

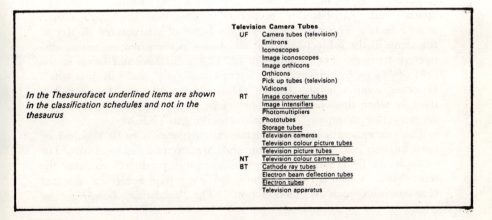

that the term is also a species of the genus "Television apparatus" and that it has other related terms which might be searched, such as "Phototubes" or "Television cameras".

If, on the other hand, the user wishes to approach the system from a broad subject point of view, he may find it more convenient to use the classification initially. He might start, for example, at M "Electronic engineering" and proceed via MA "Electron tubes" to the display for MC "Cathode ray tubes", noting MCE "Television camera tubes" among other terms of interest for information searching. He should then turn to the thesaurus entry for more details about these terms if required.

The Classification schedules

The classification groups the main subject fields in an overall structure, to give a broad view of the extent and juxtaposition of the subject areas. At the same time it shows fundamental facet divisions within the major disciplines and within these it gives displays of the main hierarchical and other relationships between the terms.

Traditionally, facet schemes break down the subject fields into fundamental categories. In the case of *Thesaurofacet* which covers so many fields in technology, it was decided to retain conventional disciplines as main headings and to analyse facets within each discipline (23). The synopsis of the main headings is given in fig. 11. In the CIRIA thesaurus the field of the construction industry is immediately divided into fundamental facets, but this is quite feasible, as the thesaurus is concerned with only one central subject area and related fields.

Within each field in *Thesaurofacet* the terms are displayed according to facet principles. This means that the nature of the concepts is examined and sorted into homogenous groups according to well-defined characteristics (see fig. 12, Glass Technology, fig. 13, Driers).

In a given subject-field, facet analysis is used to group the terms into fundamental facets or categories. These range from "Entities": "things", "parts" and "Attributes": "properties", "processes" to "Applications" and "Effects". These divisions form the bones of a structured display of the terms in the subject-field and are shown in the schedules with a distinctive typeface. For example, in fig. 12 the fundamental facets in the field of "Glass technology" are "By raw materials" and "By products". However, some schedules are not divided by fundamental facets; this is the case when the whole subject-field falls within the same fundamental category (for example, "Electrical measurements" XR).

The concepts within the fundamental categories may be grouped by facet analysis into sub-facets before they are grouped hierarchically. For example, in fig. 12 the fundamental category "products" contains the term "glass", which is further subdivided into groups according to stated characteristics, such as "composition". The "subdivide" headings, like

Fig. 11. THESAUROFACET: SYNOPSIS OF MAIN HEADINGS

A	**General concepts**
B	**Science**
BA	Mathematical sciences
C	Physics
E	Particle physics
F	Chemistry
G	Materials
I	Space sciences
IA	Earth sciences
IP	Biological science
J	**Technology**
J2	Engineering
J3	Electrical engineering
L	Circuits
M	Electronic engineering
MR	Communication engineering
O	Mechanical engineering
Q	Mechanical components
R	Transport engineering
RF	Aerospace engineering
S	Nuclear engineering
SH	Military engineering
SJ	Mining
SL	Civil engineering
SS	Environmental engineering
SY	Domestic appliances
T	Industrial engineering
TA	Production engineering
U	Metals technology
UF	Chemical technology
VU	Agriculture
W	Common technological processes
W2	Systems engineering
W5	Control systems
WG	Navigation
WJ	Data processing
WR	Reprography
X	Measurement
YK	Testing
Z	**Sociological Environment**
ZA	Management studies
ZI	Management environmental studies

the fundamental facet headings, are printed in the schedules in a distinctive type face.

Terms within the subfacets and fundamental facets are arranged in hierarchies and arrays. For example, in fig. 12 the terms UTM "Silica glass" to UTT "Devitrified glass".

Fundamental facet headings and subfacet headings are sometimes assumed to be present and are not actually stated in the schedules. This has happened in schedules where there are a few terms and the display would appear to be overloaded with facet subdivisions if all were listed.

FIG. 12. THESAUROFACET: GLASS TECHNOLOGY SCHEDULES

UTG	**GLASS TECHNOLOGY**
	*Ceramics and glass industries ZKN
	By raw materials:
UTH	Glass raw materials
	Combine with notation from minerals and inorganic substances for example:—
	*Cobalt oxide HR2/HNE
	*Silicon dioxide HIB/HNG
	By products:
UTL	Glass
	Subdivide by composition:
UTM	Silica glass
UTN	Lead glass
UTP	Phosphate glass
UTQ	Flint glass
UTS	Borosilicate glass
UTT	Devitrified glass
	Subdivide by property:
UTU	Heat resistant glass
UTW	Frosted glass
UTY	Stained glass
	Subdivide by manufactured form:
UU2	Plate glass
UU3	Sheet glass
UU5	Laminated glass
UUB	Glass fibres
UUC	Glass wool
UUD	Glass cloth
UUE	Glass tape
UUJ	Glass particles
	Subdivide by purpose:
UUL	Optical glass
UUN	Window glass
UUP	Glassware
	By process:
UUR	Glass manufacturing processes
UUS	Glass blowing

The notation

The notation consists of capital letters and numerals (omitting the numerals 0 and 1). Except in the "Classification of Business Studies" (schedule Z) the notation is ordinal and not hierarchical. This means that the notation is not structured and does not reflect subdivisions and hierarchies; this is shown instead by indentation of the terms and by facet and subfacet guide headings. For example, in fig. 14 the notation

Fig. 13. THESAUROFACET: DRIERS SCHEDULES AND THESAURUS

SCHEDULES	THESAURUS

SCHEDULES

OV **DRIERS**
    * Air conditioners OXE
    * Columns (process) URB
    * Dehumidification OX4
    * Dehumidifiers OXP
    * Dehydration OXQ
    * Demisters UKH
    * Driers (domestic) SYF
    * Drying UKB
    * Evaporators OQ
    * Furnaces OT
    * Heaters OO
    * Kilns OTQ
    * Mufflers OTR

By operating media:
OV2 Direct heat driers
OV3 Indirect heat driers
OV5 Vacuum driers

By operating time conditions:
OVA Continuous driers
    * Conveyer driers OVO
    * Drum driers OVJ
    * Moving load driers OVV
    * Tunnel truck driers OVX
OVB Batch driers
    * Tray driers OVN

By mode of action
OVD Rotary driers
    * Drum driers OVJ
    * Spin driers SYJ
    * Tumbler driers SYK
OVF Vibrating driers
OVG Agitated driers

By design and construction:
OVJ Drum driers
OVL Conical driers
OVN Tray driers
OVO Conveyer driers
OVP Belt conveyor driers
OVR Screw conveyor driers
OVT Trough driers
OVV Moving load driers
OVW Tower driers
OVX Tunnel truck driers
OVY Jacketed driers

By method of heating:
Combine with notation for Heaters, for example:
OV/OOK Electric driers
OV/OOL Dielectric seat driers

THESAURUS

Dressing Off (casting)
UF Fettling (casting)
    Shake out (casting)
    Trimming (casting)

Dried Foods
RT Drying

Driers
UF Dryers
RT Air conditioners
    Columns (process)
    Dehumidification
    Dehumidifiers
    Dehydration
    Demisters
    Drying
    Evaporators
    Furnaces
    Heaters
    Kilns
    Muffles
NT(A) Driers (domestic)
BT(A) Chemical engineering equipment

Driers (domestic)
UF Domestic driers
BT(A) Driers

Drift
RT Accuracy
    Errors
NT(A) Carrier drift
    Drift (circuits)
BT(A) Performance criteria
    (measurement)

Drift (circuits)
RT Carrier drift
    Drift corrected amplifiers
BT(A) Drift
    Network parameters

Drift Channel use
Carrier Drift

Drift Corrected Amplifiers
UF Low drift amplifiers
    Temperature compensated amplifiers
RT Drift (circuits)

Drifters use
Trawlers

Drift Meters

Drift Mobility use
Carrier Drift

Drift Path use
Carrier Drift

for "Conveyor driers" is OVO; but the notation for "Belt conveyor driers" is OVP and not OVOA as it might have been in a hierarchical system. An ordinal notation gives greater "hospitality" (ability to accommodate additional terms at any point in the schedule) and at the same time gives a shorter notation than a hierarchical system.

For machine searching the ordinal notation appears to be less satisfactory than the hierarchical, as the search programme needs to be more detailed to compensate for the lack of structure in the notation. For example C12.8 + in the MeSH "Tree structures" would bring out 'Dermatitis" and all subdivisions, whereas PKC + in *Thesaurofacet* would retrieve "Compressors" but not species of compressors, since the notation for these is covered PKD to PKW. The search programme must include instructions accordingly. One difficulty of a multipurpose system is that a notation suitable for machine retrieval is not suitable for shelf arrangement; the one needs to be structured, the length being of less importance, whilst the other requires brevity and mnemonic qualities.

The Thesaurus

The Thesaurus serves as an index to the schedules, but also controls synonyms and word forms in the manner of conventional thesauri.

Polyhierarchies

The main hierarchical relationships are shown in the schedules, and so the thesaurus does not include these in the form of BT/NT relationships. It does, however, show additional or auxiliary hierarchies and uses the symbols BT(A) and NT(A) to indicate these. For example, in fig. 14

Hydraulic servomotors   WEF

BT(A)   Hydraulic motors

The entry "Hydraulic servomotors" in the thesaurus indicates that the term is located in the "Servocomponents" schedule WE, subordinate to "Servomotors". It also indicates that the term in addition is a species of "Hydraulic motors". Checking the broader terms in the thesaurus, it will be found that "Hydraulic motors" appear at PE2 in the schedule for "Fluid power devices".

Polyhierarchies are handled rather differently by the MeSH Thesaurus and by the CIRIA Thesaurus (see fig. 8). "Plank floors" for example are placed at J9126 under "Self centering floors", but also at J9207 under "Slab floors". Both class numbers are listed in the thesaurus

PLANK FLOORS   J9126

J9207

Fig. 14. THESAUROFACET: HYDRAULIC SERVOMOTORS
SCHEDULES AND THESAURUS

	SCHEDULES		THESAURUS	
PD	**FLUID POWER DEVICES**	**Hydraulic Power Transmission Systems**		**Q5A**
	(UF common attributes 'fluid powered'.)	RT	Fluid power engineering	
	* Fluidic devices PR2	NT(A)	Hydraulic brakes	
	* Fluidic valves PL		Hydraulic clutches	
PD2	**Hydraulic equipment**		Hydraulic couplings	
PD3	Hydraulic fluids	BT(A)	Hydraulic operated devices	
PD4	Hydraulic accumulators	**Hydraulic Presses**		**TAM/PE**
PD5	Diaphragm hydraulic accumulators	*Synth*		
		RT	Hydraulic accumulators	
PD6	Piston hydraulic accumulators		Hydraulic cylinders	
			Hydraulic rams	
PDB	Boosters (hydraulic)	S BT	Presses	
PDC	Differential pistons	S BT(A)	Hydraulic operated devices	
PDH	Hydraulic reservoirs	**Hydraulic Rams**		**QIF**
PDJ	Hydraulic cylinders	RT	Hydraulic presses	
PE	Hydraulic operated devices	BT(A)	Hydraulic operated devices	
	(UF common attribute 'Hydraulic'.)	**Hydraulic Reservoirs**		**PDH**
	See thesaurus entry for	UF	Reservoirs (hydraulic)	
	individual devices.	**Hydraulic Seals**		**QMV**
PE2	Hydraulic motors	BT(A)	Hydraulic operated devices	
	* Hydraulic servomotors WEF	**Hydraulic Servomotors**		**WEF**
	* Hydraulic starters WEQ	RT	Hydraulic control systems	
PE4	Positive displacement	BT(A)	Hydraulic motors	
	hydraulic motors		Hydraulic operated devices	
PE6	Rotary hydraulic motors	**Hydraulic Shapers**		**TRH/PE**
PE7	Gear rotary hydraulic motors	*Synth*		
		S BT	Shapers	
WE	**SERVOCOMPONENTS**	S BT(A)	Hydraulic operated devices	
	* Electric control equipment JV	**Hydraulic Starters**		**WEQ**
	* Fluidic devices PR2	UF	Starter motors (hydraulic)	
	* Fluid valves PL	RT	Starting	
	* Flying controls RS2	BT(A)	Hydraulic motors	
	* Guidance components WIT		Hydraulic operated devices	
	* Servoamplifiers K4	**Hydraulic Steering Gear**		**QG9/PE**
	* Switches K4	*Synth*		
	* Temperature control instruments XQS	S BT(A)	Hydraulic operated devices	
		S BT	Steering gear	
	* Transducers XB	**Hydraulic Test Tunnels** *use*		
WE2	**Controllers**	**Water Tunnels**		
	* Electric controllers JV2	**Hydraulic to Fluidic Transducers**		**PU6**
	* Temperature control instruments XQS	**Hydraulic Turbines** *use*		
WE3	Mechanical controllers	**Water Turbines**		
WE4	Hydraulic controllers	**Hydraulic Valves**		**PLE**
WE5	Pneumatic controllers	NT(A)	Hydraulic gate valves	
	Combine with notation from appropriate schedule for variables controlled, for example:—	BT(A)	Hydraulic operated devices	
		Hydrazine Compounds		**HKC**
WE2/WCS	Pressure controllers	**Hydrazine Nitrate**		**HKC/HK6**
WEB	**Servomotors**	*Synth*		
	* Electric servomotors JLK	S BT	Hydrazine compounds	
	* Hall effect synchros KWP	S BT(A)	Nitrates	
WED	Mechanical servomotors	**Hydrazoic Acid**		**HK8**
WEF	Hydraulic servomotors			
WEH	Pneumatic servomotors	**Hydrazines**		**HKB**

This technique could have been used by *Thesaurofacet*. The auxiliary hierarchy class numbers could have been marked with an asterisk, to distinguish them from the main class numbers for shelf arrangement and classified catalogues.

Thesaurofacet does, however, show some additional hierarchies and related terms in the schedules as well as in the thesaurus. In fig. 14, for example, "Hydraulic servomotors" is shown with an asterisk under "Hydraulic motors" but the term is not given an alternative class number. These cross-references in the schedules are not made consistently, but only where it was felt that the display in the schedules would otherwise be patently incomplete.

Related terms

Terms related other than hierarchically, for example, by "whole/part" or "process/equipment", and "thing/property" relationships, are shown in the thesaurus, when these cannot be displayed in the facet schedules. For example, "Hydraulic presses" (fig. 14) is given in the thesaurus as a related term (RT) to "Hydraulic rams", because these terms are separated in the schedules, one under "presses" at TAM/PE and the other with "Jacks" at QIF. On the other hand, there is no need to relate "Plasma", "Plasma technology", "Plasma measurement techniques" and "Plasma properties and phenomena" in the thesaurus, because the relationship between these terms is clearly shown in the schedules for "Plasma physics" (Schedule ET).

Construction techniques

There are two schools of thought on the role of classification in thesaurus construction. One holds that the classification comes first and the terms are either checked against it or arise from it. Eleanor Dym, J.G. Mulvihill and D.J. Campbell have demonstrated how grouping terms under broad facets during thesaurus construction may reveal gaps in subject coverage and duplication of concepts. The CIRIA thesaurus is an example of thesaurus terms being derived wholly from a faceted classification scheme. The other school of thought argues that the terms themselves come first and when they are well defined and tabulated they "make their own classification". Gertrude London's work on a Classed thesaurus on meteorology (19, 20) demonstrates this approach. Terms were taken from glossaries, the network of relationships examined, and from these data a classification evolved. (See Fig. 15) Derek Austin's method of construction of the *British National Bibliography* thesaurus is based on a similar philosophy.

Both these approaches were used during the compilation of *Thesaurofacet*. The subject field was divided into temporary main classes and subdivisions. In more than half of these main classes, thesaurus forms (see fig. 16) were completed for the terms before the classification was

FIG. 15. GERTRUDE LONDON'S "CLASSED THESAURUS"

VISIBILITY

PHOTOMETRIC CONCEPTS (cont.)

Luminous flux density *un* illuminance	AGM 351.05
Illumination 2 -illuminance-	AGM 299.14

Luminous energy
  light energy *sy*
    -visible radiation-
    se luminous efficiency
  light energy *sy*
	AGM 351.03
	
	AGM 340.05

Illuminance
  -luminous flux-
  -irradiance-
  -light 1-
  -luminous efficiency-
  -illumination 2-
  'luminous flux density
  -luminance-
  -reflection-
  cf luminous intensity
	AGM 299.13

Luminance
  brightness *sy*
    -photometry-
    -luminous intensity-
    -illuminance-
    -extinction-
    cf luminous emittance
    -light-
    -electromagnetic radiation-
    -radiance-
    se apparent luminance
    se Lambert's law
	AGM 350.10

brightness *sy* Luminance	AGM 079.02

Luminous density
  -luminous energy-
  -radiant density-
  se luminous efficiency
  cf flux density
  cf illuminance
	AGM 350.16

developed. The forms gave details of synonyms, hierarchies and related terms, and the facet schedules were based on this information. In the remaining subject fields, a classification was produced before the thesaurus forms were completed. There were advantages in both systems, but on the whole, the thesaurus-before-schedule technique was preferable, as the facet schedules derived from the thesaurus forms benefited from the detailed picture of the concepts to be classified, particularly regarding auxiliary hierarchies and related terms. It was noticeable that facet schedules produced prior to the thesaurus forms were lacking in data on the type of relationships which cut across facet grouping, for example, between "frequency" and "frequency measurement". These relationships had to be added later, and were not always easy to discern in a post-classification situation.

Whichever of the two approaches was taken first, the point would arise when there was interaction between classification and thesaurus construction techniques, and when this happened, the result was always a clearer picture of the nature of the concept, its relationships and its place in the system.

Updating

The necessity for stringent economies during the compilation of *Thesaurofacet* meant that mechanisation of the construction process was not possible. Now that the need to update *Thesaurofacet* is becoming pressing, the lack of mechanised aids is causing concern. The AEI/English Electric Library, Whetstone, has passed over the responsibility of updating *Thesaurofacet* to the School of Information Science, Leeds Polytechnic, where the Thesaurofacet Unit has been formed for that purpose. It is hoped the Unit will operate a limited amending and updating service as an interim measure. Should funds be forthcoming, the Unit would like to put the original volume into machine-readable form to facilitate large-scale updating.

Because of the synthetic features of *Thesaurofacet,* a large number of new concepts may be added by combining existing terms, although many new concepts will have to be enumerated and inserted in the appropriate place in the notation. Here, the non-hierarchical nature of the notation has its advantages, as it is more hospitable than a hierarchical notation. In some schedules of *Thesaurofacet,* synthesis is expressly recommended and examples are included, for instance in the schedules for "Oscillators" (see fig. 17). Synthesis is also important in schedules for "Nuclear reactors" (S4), "Inorganic compounds" (H), "Elements" (G), and "Circuits" (L). Also, the "Common Attributes" schedules (AA) provide a synthetic tool which may be used throughout the scheme to express concepts containing general terms such as "size", "shape", "quantity" or "arrangement". Synthesis is being used for updating, even where it is not specifically recommended. When concepts are built up in this way, the thesaurus entry should show the combined class number, the constituent terms and also any related terms or synonyms. The newly sythesised concept should also be shown in the classified schedules.

Fig. 16. THESAUROFACET: THESAURUS FORM

Term	Facet Class Number	Associated Terms	Nature of Relationship			
			UF	NT	BT	RT
COLPITTS OSCILLATORS						
Scope notes						
Graf. An electron-tube oscillator comprising a parallel-tuned tank circuit connected between grid and plate. The tank capacitance contains two voltage dividing capacitors in series, with their capacitors in series, with their common connection at cathode potential. When these two capacitances are the plate-to-cathode and grid-to-cathode capacitances of the tube the circuit is known as an Ultra-audion oscillator.		Ultra-audion oscillators	UF			
		Feedback oscillators			BT	
		Harmonic oscillators			BT	
		Oscillators			BT	
		Power oscillators			BT	
		Tuned oscillators			BT	
Handel. An oscillator in which a tuned tank circuit is connected between grid and anode of the valve, or between base and collector of a transistor, and in which the tank capacitance is made up of two capacitors in series with their common connection at cathode or emitter potential.		Hartley oscillators				RT
		Meissner oscillators				RT
		Tuning				RT
		Tank circuits				RT

Operation of Thesaurofacet

Since *Thesaurofacet* is a multi-purpose tool, it may be used in a variety of information retrieval situations.

Pre-coordinate systems

Thesaurofacet is being used in engineering libraries in the United Kingdom for conventional classified catalogues and the shelf arrangement and filing of documents. *Thesaurofacet* is also being used as the source of terms for alphabetical printed indexes. The main problem with using *Thesaurofacet* in pre-coordinate systems is one of citation order. Traditionally, facet schedules have been operated pre-coordinately using "preferred order and chain index" techniques, the fixed citation order of facets within concepts and themes being reflected in the notation, and giving a built-in aid during practical classification. The *Thesaurofacet* does not lay down a fixed citation order, and because the main sequences of classes is "canonical" and not "faceted", the combination order — if one is used — cannot be deduced from the notation. Because of the wide scatter of related concepts it produces, especially where there is a high concentration of documents in a limited subject area, "preferred order" with chain indexing is not efficient when used for depth indexing; selective permutation is recommended as an alternative. Limited permutation should at least bring each concept to the leading place in the combined class number. The AEI/English Electric Library, Whetstone, for example, uses a "head" and "string" principle for a rotated, manually compiled depth index to report literature. For mechanised printed indexes, the descriptor form of the *Thesaurofacet* terms may be permuted or rotated according to KWIC, Double KWIC, KWOC, SLIC (21) or other techniques (22).

It is advisable to lay down a preferred citation order of concepts for the main entry of the class number prior to permutation. This is particularly important when the notation is used for document arrangement. The individual *Thesaurofacet* user organisation has to make its own decision on citation order, depending on the subject bias of the library.

Post-coordinate systems

The *Thesaurofacet* is designed so that it may be used with post-coordinate systems, whether for coordinate indexing or for computerized IR systems. When used post-coordinately, recall will be improved if the synthesized concepts are split and the constituent terms treated separately. For example LL/DYF "Microwave oscillators" should be indexed LL "Oscillators" and DYF "Microwaves". Either the class numbers or the word forms of the concepts may be used. However, a recent test on the performance of the *Thesaurofacet* class numbers,

Fig. 17. THESAUROFACET: SYNTHESIS; OSCILLATORS

SCHEDULES		THESAURUS	

SCHEDULES

LL   **OSCILLATORS**

By frequency:

Combine with notation from frequency schedules, for example:—

LL/CFQ   Audiofrequency oscillators
LL/DY2   Radiofrequency oscillators
LL/DY5   Very low frequency oscillators
LL/DYD   Very high frequency oscillators
LL/DYF   Microwave oscillators
LL/DYG   Ultrahigh frequency oscillators

By active element:

Combine notation for oscillators with notation for specific active elements and subdivisions, for example:—

LL/EX   Plasma oscillators
LL/KVW   Photoelectric oscillators
LL/MA   Electron tube oscillators
     * Transitron oscillators   LM8

For specific electron tube oscillators combine with notation from electron tube schedules, for example:—

LL/MBF   Travelling wave oscillators
LL/MBM   Magnetron oscillators
LL/MBP   Velocity modulated oscillators
LL/MBQ   Klystron oscillators
LL/MDB   Dynatron oscillators
LL/MDC   Resnatron oscillators
LL/MH   Semiconductor oscillators
     * Thermal oscillators   LNJ

For specific semiconductor oscillators combine with notation from semiconductor schedules, for example:

LL/MI6   Tunnel diode oscillators
LL/MIE   Avalanche transit time oscillators
LL/MJ   Transistor oscillators
LL/MN   Superconductor oscillators
LL/MNE   Maser oscillators
LL/MO   Laser oscillators
LL/PR   Fluidic oscillators

By power level:

LM3   Power oscillators
LM4   Micropower oscillators

THESAURUS

Microwave Mixers   **LX/DYF**
   S RT   Microwaves
   S BT   Mixers (circuits)
     BT(A)   Microwave devices

Microwave Network *use*

Microwave Communication Systems

Microwave Oscillators   **LL/DYF**
Synth
   RT   Josephson junctions
   S   Microwaves
   S BT   Oscillators
     BT(A)   Microwave devices
       Radar apparatus

Microwave Power Measurements *use*
Power Measurement (radiofrequency)

Microwave Radio Relays *use*
Microwave Communication Systems

Microwave Region *use*
Microwaves

Microwave Relay Systems *use*
Microwave Communication Systems

Microwave Resonators *use*
Cavity Resonators

Microwaves   **DYF**
   UF   Microwave frequencies
       Microwave region
   RT   Electrotherapy
       Extremely high frequencies
       Infrared radiation
       Masers
       Microwave communication systems
       Microwave devices
       Microwave measurements
       Millimeter waves
       Radio beams
       Superhigh frequency
       Tropospheric propagation
       Ultrahigh frequency
       Wave guide theory

Microwave Spectroscopy   **Y4H**
   BT(A)   Microwave devices

Microwave Transistors   **MJ/DYF**
Synth
   S BT   Microwaves
   S RT   Transistors
     BT(A)   Microwave devices

in an experimental computerized system at Cranfield, indicates that the high pre-combination level of some of the concepts may reduce recall. It is possible to overcome this by splitting a concept such as "Machine tool control" WD into "Machine tools" TA2 and "Control" W5. But since some of the constituent terms of the enumerated concepts do not have a place or a class number in the schedules, it might be preferable to use the word form of the concepts so that any concept may be reduced to its constituent words for mechanized operation.

Natural language systems

The *Thesaurofacet* is also a useful tool at the search stage in natural language and free text systems as an aid in programme compilation. It scores over the conventional faceted systems for this purpose, because it is better able to indicate synonymous terms and to display the interrelationships between pre-combined concepts and subject-fields.

Conclusions

The integration of the alphabetical and systematic approach achieved in *Thesaurofacet* may not be as original a feature as was at first claimed (24) although there is novelty in the combination of a detailed facet classification with a thesaurus. *Thesaurofacet* may more correctly be regarded as a new concept in information retrieval, because of its versatility. It was the first retrieval language designed to be adaptable to many I.R. systems, both pre-coordinate and post-coordinate. Whether a multipurpose tool is in practice more useful than one constructed with a specific application in view, will only be proved by experience in the use of *Thesaurofacet* and systems modelled upon it.

REFERENCES

1. AITCHISON, J., GOMERSALL, A. and IRELAND, R. *Thesaurofacet: a Thesaurus and Faceted Classification for Engineering and Related Subjects*. Whetstone (Leics.), English Electric Company, 1970.
2. BINNS, J. and BAGLEY, D. *A Faceted Classification for Engineering*. 3rd ed. Whetstone (Leics.), English Electric Company, 1961.
3. ENGINEERS' JOINT COUNCIL. *Thesaurus of Engineering and Scientific Terms (TEST)*. New York, 1967.
4. ROSTRON, R.M. "The Construction of a Thesaurus." *Aslib Proceedings*, v. 20, no. 3, 1968. p. 81-87.
5. INTERNATIONAL ROAD RESEARCH DOCUMENTATION. *IRRD Thesaurus*.
6. EURATOM. Centre for information and documentation. *Euratom thesaurus:* Part 2, terminology charts, 2nd ed. Brussels, 1967.

7. INTERNATIONAL ATOMIC ENERGY AUTHORITY. *Thesaurus.* Vienna, 1970.

8. LESK, M.E. *Word-word Associations in Document Retrieval Systems.* Cornell University, Department of Computer Science. 1968. (Report No. ISR-13 Section IX.)

9. SPARCK-JONES, K. *The Use of Automatically Obtained Keyword Classifications.* Final report, Cambridge, Cambridge Language Unit, 1969. (OSTI Report 5038).

10. COPPER DEVELOPMENT ASSOCIATION. *Thesaurus of Terms on Copper Technology.* 3rd ed. New York, 1966.

11. U.S. NATIONAL LIBRARY OF MEDICINE. *Medical subject headings; tree structures.*

12. DYM, E.D. "A New Approach to the Development of a Technical Thesaurus." *In: A.D.I. Levels of Interaction between Man and Information,* 1967. p. 126-161.

13. MULVIHILL, J.G. and BRENNER, E.H. "Faceted Organization of a Thesaurus Vocabulary." *In: American Documentation Institute, Annual Meeting, Santa Monica, Oct. 3-7, 1966. Proceedings.* p. 175-183.

14. BAUER, G. "Anwendung des Prinzips der Facettenklassifikation für den Aufbau von Thesauri." [Application of the principles of facet classification to thesaurus structure.] *ZIID Zeitschrift,* v. 14, no. 3, 1967. p. 72-83.

15. BAUER, G. "Zur geeigneten Begriffsordnung im Thesaurussystem Chemie." [On suitable concept arrangement in the Chemistry Thesaurus.] *Informatik,* v. 16, no. 2, 1969. p. 35-41; no. 5, p. 11-16.

16. MARLOT, L. et MOUREAU, M. *Elaboration d'un thésaurus pétrolier en français.* [Design of a petroleum thesaurus in French.] Paris, Centre National de la Recherche Scientifique, Centre de Documentation, 1970.

17. CONSTRUCTION INDUSTRY RESEARCH AND INFORMATION ASSOCIATION. *Thesaurus for the construction industry;* compiled by Michael Roberts and others. 1st draft, 1970.

18. CROGHAN, A. *Thesaurus-classification for non-book materials.* London, The Author, 1970.

19. LONDON, G. *A Classed Thesaurus as an Aid for Indexing, Classifying and Searching.* Report for the period July 1965 - July 1966. New Brunswick, N.J. Rutgers—The State University, Graduate School of Library Science, 1966 (PB 73 954).

20. LONDON, G. "Glossary-Based Classed Thesauri as the Core of a Modular Reference System." *In: International Forum on Informatics,* Moscow, 1969, v. 2, p. 286-315.

21. SHARP, J.R. "The SLIC index" *In: Looking Forward in Documentation; proceedings of the 38th annual conference, Exeter, 1964.* London, Aslib, 1964, p. 2-11 to 2-16. *Also in: American Documentation,* v. 17, no. 1, Jan. 1966, p. 41-4.

22. DOWELL, N.G. and MARSHALL, J.W. "Experiences with Computer-produced Indexes." *Aslib Proceedings,* Oct. 1962, p. 323-32.

23. AITCHISON, J. "Practical Application of a Facet Classification, with Special Reference to the English Electric Faceted Classification for Engineering." *In: Bakewell, K.G.B. ed. Classification for Information Retrieval,* London, Bingley, 1968. p. 55-56.

24. AITCHISON, J. "Thesaurofacet: a multipurpose retrieval language tool." *Journal of Documentation.* v. 26, no. 3, 1970, p. 187-203.

DISCUSSION

Mr. *Freeman* asked if Mrs. Aitchison could give some information on the development of the INSPEC thesaurus.

Mrs. *Aitchison* first explained that INSPEC was an organization created to produce *Science Abstracts* by computer and to provide mechanized SDI and information retrieval services based on *Science Abstracts*. Natural language terms were being used for indexing but a thesaurus was being prepared as a tool to assist in the searching procedures. Natural language terms selected by the indexers were checked against the thesaurus to identify the equivalent controlled-language terms and then listed as new entry-terms. Terms for which no appropriate thesaurus terms exist were entered into the thesaurus hierarchies as appropriate. This thesaurus generation process was computer-assisted and would shortly be on-line.

In response to another question on the possible obsolescence of *Thesaurofacet*, Mrs. Aitchison said that obsolescence was a problem and that, possibly, if the system had been purely faceted it might not become out of date so rapidly. However, if *Thesourofacet* was used in an SDI system there was a probability that obsolescence would not be so great a problem, since each run-off presents new problems in any case.

Mr. *Shumway* commented on the problems of machine systems, noting especially that updating a thesaurus raised problems of retrospective file maintenance and of retrospective searching. He further said that, in the past, MeSH had been limited to four levels of specificity and that this was to be increased to seven levels. However, getting down to this level of specificity raised many intellectual problems. On the question of codes he noted that the National Library of Medicine used codes for the machine system different from those which were used for shelf arrangement of books.

Mrs. *Aitchison* said that she appreciated the latter problem in large systems but believed that in small installations it was possible to use the same codes for both purposes.

THE *PRECIS* SYSTEM FOR COMPUTER-GENERATED INDEXES AND ITS USE IN THE *BRITISH NATIONAL BIBLIOGRAPHY*

Derek Austin

OSTI/PRECIS Project
British National Bibliography

A logical extension of the theory of faceted classification is considered from the viewpoints of (a) shelf order classifications and (b) machine-based retrieval systems. A general citation order formula which holds throughout the subject spectrum is not regarded as feasible for a shelf order scheme, but becomes a practical proposition from the viewpoint of machine-held files. A general decision-making model for regulating citation order, based on the syntax of English, is now being developed at the British National Bibliography. Its application to PRECIS is described, and its use as the basis for a multi-system authority file is considered.

I feel I should start by making a small but important point concerning the status of PRECIS as a computer-generated subject index. In the strict sense of the words, this index is not generated by a computer. Although we use the machine to reduce the clerical drudgery of manipulating index terms and filing entries and references, it will be seen that both the verbal content and the format of an index entry, as well as the complementary hierarchies of "See" and "See also" references, are entirely dependent upon human intellectual decisions. We are not, therefore, engaged in computerised indexing as this is sometimes understood so much as in developing and using a decision-making model which allows us to make a reasonable use of machine assistance.

Before we get down to what might be called the anatomy and physiology of a PRECIS index, we should first consider briefly some of the stages in its evolution, and see how these relate to the classification research which Tom Wilson reported in his paper. Although we are concerned with the manipulation of English words and phrases, not with a system of notation, PRECIS has nevertheless developed directly out of those techniques of faceted classification and relational analysis which were described this morning, and I like to think of the development of this index as part of the continuing search for a new general classification.

It could be said that modern classification theory has been built upon two relatively simple propositions. The first is that any compound subject, no matter how complex, can be broken down into its separate parts or concepts, any one of which may need to be considered as an access point to the subject as a whole. Secondly, the theory suggests that once a subject has been broken into its separate components in this way, it can then be reconstructed to a standard and consistent pattern by referring to some kind of decision-making model. A number of these models or citation order formulae have now been developed, but the overall strategy of analysing a subject into its parts, then a check against a formula, followed by a restructuring of the subject, remains a common feature of all analytico-synthetic classifications.

This approach to classification suggests that we should be able to construct a general classification by extending these two propositions to their logical limits. Since every subject is made up of separate elements which have independent existence as conceptions in their own right, it should theoretically be possible to code each concept once-and-for-all with a single piece of notation which would allow us to retrieve it from any of the subjects in which it has occurred. The technique also suggests that it should be possible to establish a logically predictable order of terms which holds good across the entire spectrum of knowledge, so that when we are dealing with books on politics we would use a subject-building model which is just as valid in the fields of, say, chemistry and music.

It is true that analytico-synthetic techniques are employed in faceted classifications such as UDC and the Colon Classification, and the origin of these techniques can be traced back even further to the first use of common subdivisions in the Dewey Decimal Classification (DC) but no scheme has so far been constructed which adopts such a completely generalised approach to the organisation of knowledge. This would amount to assigning every concept in the index of the DC to its tables of common subdivisions, then using a common set of rules to build all the subjects we handle out of these separate elements as and when each subject is encountered.

The reason this has not been attempted is fairly clear, and has to be related to the principal function of a documentary classification, which is to organise libraries as collections of physical objects. If each separate element in a compound subject had to be identified by its own unique piece of notation, the class numbers for all but the simplest subjects would inevitably become so long and cumbersome that they could never be used as shelving marks. Even a faceted scheme like UDC makes some concessions to this fact, and achieves a large measure of economy by using what might be called subject expressive notation rather than concept identifying codes. For example, the material "Iron" is represented by at least seven different class numbers in UDC, each one of which conveys quite a complicated packet of information.

The use of a classification scheme to organise library stock also has a bearing on the feasibility of a universal citation order. However desirable this might seem from a classifier's point of view, it hardly needs saying that for library organisation purposes a citation order which seems to be most appropriate in one field of knowledge, such as "Politics", is most unlikely to be equally effective when we are dealing with works on, say, "Chemistry" and "Criminology". Indeed, from this particular viewpoint it is doubtful whether we should ever be able to develop an entirely logical model for regulating the order of concepts which proves to be equally satisfactory across the entire subject spectrum. It is notable that the best known model of this kind, the PMEST formula of Dr. Ranganathan, cannot be used at all until the classifier has already assigned a subject in his mind to some main class or other. This means that a particular factor in a compound subject has had to be pre-selected as its most significant concept from a shelving point of view before the classifier can even use the model to determine the order in which the remaining elements should be cited, usually in some order of decreasing significance from the viewpoint of the classification scheme in use.

However, we face an entirely different situation when we are dealing with machine-held subject files. The computer has no aesthetic scruples, and it is not at all concerned about the length of a class number, while in terms of machine economics it would obviously be more satisfactory if a single conception such as 'Iron' could be identified for retrieval purposes by the same piece of notation no matter where it occurs in the file. We have been studying this question of coding for machine retrieval in the Classification Research Group in London. As Tom Wilson has explained, we turned away from the idea of a subject expressive notation, and explored instead the idea of coding each specific concept on a once-and-for-all basis, ready for use in building any compound subject. We intend, however, that these codes should be more than just randomly assigned labels, and we hope in time to develop a system of hierarchically expressive notation which shows how each concept belongs to certain categories of semantically related ideas. It should then be possible to use the computer to browse up and down a hierarchy of concepts related by their meanings, so that we virtually add a second dimension to any machine-based search. These categories would finally be organised into a general thesaurus covering the whole of knowledge, and this would serve as the concept source when we come to build subjects out of their component parts.

Assuming that concepts can be organised and notated in this way — and we have found no reasons for supposing that this cannot be done — the act of classifying would consist of three separate stages. In the first place, a subject would be analysed into its parts, and these would be located in the thesaurus and translated into pieces of notation. A decision-making model based on various relationships between concepts would next be checked to determine the order in which these parts should be written down as a subject string—I shall return to this point more fully later on. Finally, this string would be keyboarded and input to a machine-held file, together with any associated document codes or shelving marks which indicate where the document itself or an appropriate citation can be located. Any enquiries we put to the system would be translated into strings of notated elements in the same way, and the machine would be set to search through the files looking for a match or a near-match between the terms of an enquiry and the items in the store. I should perhaps make the point here and now that although this system may give us the ability to construct subjects freely and to any necessary depth as they are encountered, and although we could use it for retrieving subject data in ways which go beyond the capacity of any shelf order system, we realise that it has also become practically unusable for shelf ordering purposes. Nor is it intended for this function. I have come to doubt whether we shall ever be able to design a completely successful scheme which will serve at one and the same time for both library organisation and for the retrieval of specific concepts from a machine-held file. Each of these different systems has its task to perform and its own special criteria to meet, and each of them merits its own theoretical approach to the organisation of knowledge.

This matter of searching machine-held files raised an interesting question which, as it turned out, had a direct bearing on the development of PRECIS. Once a compound subject has been translated into a string of machine-readable codes, we next have to consider the pros and cons of the various ways in which we can store this string in the computer. We first, and perhaps naturally, considered filing it as it stood under its first coded element, much as we shelve a book under the class number which represents its most significant concept. This would keep the file down to a reasonable size, since each string would be entered on the file only once, but it would also entail a lengthy searching routine, since the machine would have to examine the file from beginning to end if we wished to identify all the citations in which some specific concept or combination of concepts had occurred, simply because they could have appeared in any part of a string.

An alternative method was suggested to us by the data processing team engaged on the British MARC Project. This was to program the machine so that each string, as it is accepted into the system, is reconstructed by the computer in a series of steps which brings each of its significant terms in succession to the front of the string. The whole of the subject would then be filed in turn under each of its significant concepts, but in such a way that its original relationships would be preserved.

We should, of course, require a large file capacity if we intended to store the same subject in several places in this way, and a single compound subject may need to be filed in as many different places as there are significant concepts in its structure. Against this question of file capacity, however, we weighed the obvious gains we should make in terms of faster access, since we could then locate a subject in its entirety under any of its significant terms. In addition to this, we would have created a further facility to scan quickly and at one place the various different contexts in which our chosen term had appeared. Faced with the choice between a small store with slow access and a larger store with faster access, it seems that computer people will tend to prefer speed every time. We were assured that the capacity of computer-held files is being continually improved, so that this no longer constitutes a major factor in assessing computer use, but it also seems that processing time is likely to remain a relatively expensive item.

At about this time the *British National Bibliography* started to explore the possibility of producing its printed-page subject index from a single string of subject descriptors taken from the MARC magnetic tapes, and as part of this research we carried out some experiments in rotating strings of concepts in this way. We were, of course, now using English words rather than bits of notation to represent the parts of a compound subject, but the general technique was the same, and from this point on it will be difficult to draw any clear distinction between classification and verbal subject indexing. In any case, no attempt has yet been made to establish a final scheme of notation.

Almost immediately we ran into unexpected difficulties, and these could only be attributed to the ways in which we had been organising terms into strings. There seem to be no particular problems in instructing a computer to rotate a string of terms so that each one comes in turn to the lead position, and in most cases we found that we could then read and understand the entries which were produced, no matter which of the terms in the string was serving as the access word. In some cases, however, the subject statement turned out to be decidedly ambiguous when we tried to construct index entries under any term except the first one in the string, while in certain extreme examples we found that we had lost the meaning of the subject altogether.

We had been organising terms into strings according to certain ordering rules which were associated with a system of relational operators. Each operator consisted of a number which was written in front of a term to specify the role it played in a particular subject. For example, we would write one number in front of an activity concept, but a different number to specify the agent of the action if this was also present. Each number possessed its own filing value which then ensured that terms would be organised into a standard and consistent pattern when we came to reconstruct the subject out of its parts. Even in a machine-based system some kind of predetermined order is necessary, not only to ensure that enquiries put to the system match the subjects already on the file, but also to distinguish clearly between the different subjects which can be made out of the same basic ideas.

The particular set of operators which led to these ambiguous entries had been developed during research into a dual-purpose classification—that is, one which is intended for library organisation as well as for machine retrieval. As a result, these operators gave us an order of terms which was supposed to reflect their relative significance as shelving factors, so that concepts which appeared to be more important from this point of view came earlier in the string. For example, concepts such as Space and Time had been given a low filing value which indicated their relative insignificance from a shelving point of view, and it had not seemed necessary to take any account of the effect which this might have on the meaningfulness of a subject statement. It is also notable that no operator at all had been allocated to the first concept in a string. This was called, quite vaguely, the "principal concept", and the choice of whichever subject factor appeared to fill this role was left to the indexer, and could vary according to the subject field being indexed. In fact, we had made no serious attempt to establish an entirely logical model for ordering terms into strings which applied throughout the scheme.

It was some time before I realised that this idea of organising terms according to their significance as shelving factors was not only responsible for the loss of meaning in some of our rotated index entries, but that it simply has no part to play in the kind of machine-held subject files we were trying to develop. We were, after all, planning to rotate the parts of a subject so that any term we selected would come in due course into the lead position. Once in this position, it would automatically acquire the status of the "most significant" concept in that particular entry. The important thing then was to make quite sure that the meaning of the subject had not become lost or distorted during this process of rotation, and it was from this new point of view that I started to re-examine the whole question of citation order.

A clue to this question of meaningfulness came from a study of the different entries we had produced up to that time. These showed that we could preserve the correct meaning of a set of index entries throughout a series of rotations providing that each term in the original string was directly related to the next term or terms regardless of their relative significance, much as the words in an English sentence form a linear sequence based on the syntactic relations of object, verb and subject. We also found that we could get consistent and encouraging results if we wrote terms down in such an order that one term established the wider context in which the next term had been considered by the author. Supposing, for example, that we were indexing a document on "The management of railways in France". In this case it is the locality "France" which sets the whole subject into its widest context, and despite its obvious lack of value as a shelving factor this word is nevertheless set down as the first element in the string. We would next write "Railways" as the term which is context-established by "France", while the verb-noun "Management" would be set down last on the grounds that it is the railways which are being managed, not the country in which they occur.

The logic which underlies this order can be demonstrated with the following simple diagram which shows a narrowing of context as we read from left to right:

$$A \; > \; B \; > \; C \; > \; D$$

That is, the author has considered the concept D in the context of C, C in the context of B, and B in the context of A. This corresponds, very roughly, to the order of words found in the passive sentence in English.

If this string of concepts is now considered from the special viewpoint of one of its middle terms — the concept C for example — it will be found that the string breaks down naturally into three separate parts according to this idea of context dependence:

$$\boxed{A \; B \cdot} \; \longmapsto \; \boxed{C} \; \longmapsto \; \boxed{D}$$

If we count the concept C as the first part and consider this as the user's point of entry to the index, it will be seen that this term is related to the rest of the entry in two different ways. Any terms appearing to the left of C form a second group which set the entry word into its wider context, while the terms to the right of C — that is, D in this example — form another group which are context-dependent on C itself.

These three groups of concepts form the main structural components of a typical PRECIS entry, and terms are coded at a later stage so that the computer can recognize the group or groups to which each term should be addressed when it starts to construct a set of entries out of a single string of words. Potentially, any entry in PRECIS can have terms assigned to these three basic positions, though they are not always occupied. These positions, which we call the Lead, the Qualifier and the Display, can also be demonstrated in the form of a diagram, with the three basic parts of an entry arranged as they appear on the printed page:

$$\boxed{\text{LEAD}} \qquad \boxed{\text{Qualifier}}$$
$$\boxed{\textit{Display}}$$

The special role which each of these three positions plays in conveying meaning to the user can be shown more easily if we look at a typical set of index entries:

HOSPITALS. United States
Personnel management. Application of computer systems
  Conference proceedings

PERSONNEL MANAGEMENT. Hospitals. United States
Application of computer systems - *Conference proceedings*

COMPUTER SYSTEMS. Application in personnel management.
  Hospitals. United States
Conference proceedings

Taking the second entry as an example, it can be seen that the lead position is occupied by the term "Personnel management". This is the concept which we anticipate will be looked up by the user who is interested in this subject, and the words are printed in bold type and are set out from the rest of the entry for easier location on the page. The wider context of this concept is then established by words in a different type face in the Qualifier position—first by the word "Hospitals", and then by the place element "United States". It should be noted that when terms move into the Qualifier position the computer prints them in the reverse of their original order, so that the context now becomes progressively wider rather than narrower as we read from left to right. The Display position, which is indented below on a second line, is occupied by the prepositional phrase "Application of computer systems", followed by the form statement, *"Conference proceedings"*, which is printed in italic. This change of type face is introduced to show a fundamental change of relationships—we can recognise that the concept "Personnel management" has a direct or one-to-one relationship with the concept "Hospitals", but it is clear that the form of the document must relate to the subject as a whole, not just to the previous term. In this particular example no attempt has been made, on economic grounds, to create entries under the terms "United States", "Application" or "Conference proceedings", though these could have been generated if necessary.

These entries demonstrate some of the features which I tried to suggest when choosing a name for the system. The name PRECIS is an acronym for Preserved Context Index System, and is intended to convey this idea of context dependency as well as the fact that a summarisation of the subject — a kind of précis — is offered to the user under any word in a subject statement which has been marked as significant enough to be used as a lead term. As each of these terms comes into the lead position, the entry is restructured in such a way that the user can determine, through visual clues in its layout and its typography, both the wider context and the narrower terms which relate to his chosen approach word.

In restructuring a set of entries in this way the computer has, in fact, simply shunted the components of an initial concept string through the three basic positions we considered earlier. For example, the concept "Personnel management", which appears on the lower line of the first entry, is shifted in successive steps so that it occupies the lead position in the second entry, then moves across into the qualifier position in the final entry. Once in this position, it takes on a new relational role as part of a prepositional phrase which establishes the context in which the concept "Computer systems" has been considered.

Obviously, we do not expect an indexer to write out sets of rotated entries in this way, except as part of his training. His task is, firstly, to analyse the subject of a document into its component parts, then organise these into a string of terms suitable for machine manipulation. I mentioned earlier that the input order of terms in PRECIS corresponds roughly to the order of words in the passive sentence in English. However, this is not of its own accord precise enough to be turned into a general instruction, and instead we use a set of relational operators to ensure that terms are set down consistently in a logical order when preparing strings for input.

PRECIS: RELATIONAL OPERATORS

- (a) *Form*: Physical (e.g. Microform) or Narrative (e.g. Journal)
- (b) *Target*: e.g. *For engineering*
- (/) *Quasi-generic relationship*
- , *Difference:* e.g. concept used adjectivally
- (p) *Part, Material*
- (q) *Property, Percept*
- (0) *Study region, Sample population*
- (1) *Viewpoint, Perspective*
- (2) *Active concept*
- (3) *Effect, Action*
- (4) *Key system*
- (5) *Discipline*
- (6) *Environment*
- (v) *Coordinate concept*
- (w) *Relationship between coordinate concepts*
- (x) *Coordinate theme*

These operators are used in much the same way as the set we considered earlier. In practice, an indexer scans a document looking for those terms which he regards as essential to a verbal expression of its subject content. He next considers the role which each of these terms plays in the subject as a whole, and codes them according to their roles by writing down an appropriate operator in front of each term. Each operator has been given a special filing value which then ensures that terms are set down in the correct order for producing a set of meaningful entries.

It would hardly be appropriate to start a crash course in PRECIS indexing here and now, but at least I can try to demonstrate the use of this model by showing how it performs with a fairly straightforward subject. If we were indexing the subject we considered earlier — that is, "The management of railways in France" — we would begin by breaking this down into its three substantive elements, "France", "Management" and "Railways". We would then check each of these terms against the model to decide how it should be coded. There is a rule which states that every string must include at least one term which is coded either (3), which represents an activity, or (4), which represents a thing, much as every sentence in English must contain at least a verb and an object. In this example we can recognise "Management" as the activity concept, and we can start by coding this term:

(3) Management

The use of this code then automatically calls for the name of the entity on which the action has been performed, providing that this is present in the subject. The system being managed is, of course, "Railways", so we would next code this as (4) and label it as the key system:

(4) Railways

(3) Management

This leaves the locality "France" to be considered, and here we have to make a choice between two different codes. If the author has been studying the general problems of railway management, and states quite clearly that he worked in France only to gather case material, we should have to regard France as a study region and code it accordingly by choosing the operator (0). If, however, the document is basically a study of the French railway system, which seems to be the more likely, we would code the name of the country as (6) and label it as the environment of the main theme. These numbered codes are always filed retroactively — that is to say, in order of decreasing ordinal value — which gives us the following final order of codes and terms:

(6) France

(4) Railways

(3) Management

This is, of course, the order we established earlier when we considered this subject from the viewpoint of context dependency. After this string has been coded, the computer would produce the following entries:

FRANCE
    Railways. Management

RAILWAYS. France
    Management

MANAGEMENT. Railways. France

Most of the subjects we handle at the monograph level in the *British National Bibliography* conform to this general pattern, with terms falling into a straight-forward sequence based on their one-to-one relationships. The system of operators can, however, deal with far more complex subjects than this, including those which involve coordinate relationships in which two or more terms are simultaneously related to some common term higher up the string. These complicated subjects occur more frequently at the level of abstracts and journal articles, and we are now engaged in experimental indexing with this kind of material in a variety of different subject fields. These experiments are intended to test the system, and have led to some necessary re-thinking of our methods, but the present system has proved capable of dealing with any situation we have met so far, and since we can introduce certain operators more than once into the same string we have had no difficulty in indexing at any level of specificity.

We have also found that subjects of every kind are amenable to control from this viewpoint of context dependency. Reactions from users of the index generally confirm our opinion that quite complicated entries can be readily understood from the fact that terms have been set down in such an order that one establishes the context for another, and it seems that we are all, as readers, generally sensitive to this idea of context. However, if an indexer does detect that the order of terms is not enough of its own accord to resolve ambiguity he can bring another mechanism into play, and can introduce prepositional phrases to clarify relationships even further. These phrases are also constructed by the computer out of terms in the concept string, and we saw an example of this earlier in the entries dealing with "Hospitals", where the prepositional phrase "Application of computer systems", which appeared in the first two entries, was transformed into the phrase "Application in personnel management" in the final entry.

In the examples we have looked at so far the computer has handled terms, including those which consist of more than one word, as though they were single units for manipulation purposes. It can, however, bring any part of a noun or prepositional phrase into the lead position as necessary, and can make separate entries under any adjectives which are associated with a noun as well as under the noun itself. It does this by a process of rotation, not by inverting the heading, so that compound terms and phrases always appear on the page in their natural language order:

PLASTICS
Carbon whisker reinforced plastics

REINFORCED PLASTICS
Carbon whisker reinforced plastics

WHISKER REINFORCED PLASTICS
Carbon whisker reinforced plastics

CARBON WHISKER REINFORCED PLASTICS

Up to this point I have concentrated mostly on the organisation of words into strings according to their syntactic relationships. This still leaves us with the problem of how we should deal with words and their semantic relationships. No matter how well a subject statement has been constructed, we can never guarantee that a user is going to enter the alphabetical file under just those terms which an indexer has selected as lead words; he might, for example, begin a search from a more general term, or he might think of some alternative word which has the same meaning.

We try to allow for this by creating a separate but complementary system of references which direct the user to specific entry words from unused synonyms and other semantically related terms. These references are also generated from a computer-held file. After an index string has been written, it is checked term by term, and any necessary higher terms and other related words are established by examining dictionaries, special subject thesauri and existing classification schemes. Most of these reference tools have not been designed with our particular needs in mind, and it is a pleasure to record here our debt to the *Thesaurofacet*, of which we shall hear more later, in which terms in a number of subject fields have already been conveniently organised into semantically related categories. When the words which form the two parts of a reference have established, we assign code numbers to both the higher and the lower terms, and the terms are then input to a random access file in such a way that the correct reference will be generated automatically by the computer whenever we quote, as part of the PRECIS input, the number which identifies the term which actually appears in the lead position in an entry. Any higher term may itself, of course, be related to some next higher term, and so on up a hierarchy. These further links are also established and stored in just the same way, so that whenever we quote a code number which represents a lead term in the index the machine extracts the entire hierarchy and prints out all the necessary references without further intervention by the indexer.

In setting up these hierarchies we make no attempt to identify, as part of the reference, the exact subject in which some specific concept has occurred. Each reference therefore stands as a link between individual ideas, not between composite themes, which means that the same code can be quoted whenever that particular concept re-appears in some other subject. After only four months live working it has become clear to us that most documents, including those which claim to be the first work on some obscure topic, rarely deal with entirely original concepts; mostly they juxtapose terms which are already on our file, though sometimes in unexpected ways. At the moment we spend a good deal of our time setting up these hierarchies of semantically related terms, but already the proportion of time spent in this way is decreasing as more links are recorded and filed ready for use in building a variety of different subjects.

A PRECIS index is therefore the product of two different but interdependent teams, each of which produces input for computer-held files. The first team is concerned with organising terms into strings based on their syntactic relationships, which leads to the production of sets of index entries, while the second is engaged in building up hierarchies of references based on the semantic relationships between individual concepts, which could ultimately lead to the production of a machine-held general thesaurus. Between them, these two systems constitute all the verbal side of the index system—one of them expresses a summary statement of the subject at any level of specificity, and the other guides the user to an appropriate entry word from other terms which share an element of common meaning. But we still have to tell the reader where to find the bibliographic citations which give details of the document itself.

This is not a particular problem when we are indexing abstracts and journal articles, since the index entry can include, as a final piece of information, the abstract number or some other mark which identifies the appropriate citation. The *British National Bibliography,* however, is basically a classified catalogue, which means that a standard catalogue entry for every work is printed under an appropriate DC class number in the main section of the bibliography. In addition, *BNB* produces data for the British side of the international MARC network, so that we also have responsibility for any other classification systems which appear on the MARC record. This means that before concept strings go on to the computer section they have to be considered by two further groups of people—that is, the Decimal Classification team and the team who assign Library of Congress classification numbers and subject headings.

We have now started looking into the use of PRECIS as a means for reducing some of the work load on these different teams of indexers and classifiers. I mentioned earlier that PRECIS is able to express the subject of a document at any level of specificity, the limit being set by the contents of the document itself, not by the printed tables of a classification scheme. Perhaps not surprisingly, we have found that some 85% of the index strings we write at *BNB* exceed the class numbers of the Decimal Classification in terms of specificity. It should therefore be possible to regard the PRECIS string as a basic subject statement which is more than adequate for normal classification purposes, so that the subject of a document needs to be analysed only once. In this connection it is worth recalling that the structure of a PRECIS string is based on the syntax of English, not on some prior judgement concerning the relative significance of its different parts. This neutrality can also be put to some advantage. Since a concept analysis for PRECIS represents a full and syntactically logical statement of the subject, there should theoretically be one and only one "most logical" place to which each string can be assigned in various different shelf-order classifications, even when the string is more specific than the schedules. It might therefore be possible to use the PRECIS analysis of a subject as an intermediate link between different classification schemes, or even between different editions of the same scheme, since the subject will be represented by the same string, regardless of which of its various factors is selected as the shelving element. For example, our initial analysis of a subject we considered earlier produced the following entries:

HOSPITALS. United States
  Personnel management. Application of computer systems
  - *Conference proceedings*

PERSONNEL MANAGEMENT. Hospitals. United States
  Application of computer systems - *Conference proceedings*

COMPUTER SYSTEMS. Application in personnel management.
    Hospitals. United States
    Conference proceedings

One classification scheme may assign this subject to the class "Hospital administration", and another could place it with works on "Personnel management", while a third scheme regards it as an aspect of "Computer applications", but the string itself will remain consistently the same, and is neutral with respect to all these different viewpoints.

Over the past few months we have been experimenting with the idea of translating these neutral subject strings into their most appropriate numbers in different classification schemes, with the intention of creating a multi-system authority file for both *BNB* and MARC. It is too early yet to report any definite findings, but the results of this work look promising. We have had some difficulty with those parts of the *Library of*

Congress classification which are especially intended for the in-house organisation of stock, so that they tend to be book-specific rather than subject-specific—that is to say, they either use non-subject data as a basis for dividing documents into classes, or they set out to identify a particular edition of a particular author rather than specify subject content. This problem rarely occurs with the *Decimal Classification,* which mostly tends to be subject-specific.

This concept of a multi-system authority file starts to look like a practical proposition as soon as we recognise that we are dealing with a subject which is already on the file, since we can then use the computer to generate all the necessary data, including these various class numbers. As a document goes from one subject team to another at the *British National Bibliography,* a packet of information is built up item by item until it contains, at present, five sets of data:

(1)   the PRECIS string
(2)   the codes which generate the 'See' and 'See also' references
(3)   a *DC* class number
(4)   a *Library of Congress* class number
(5)   the appropriate *Library of Congress* subject headings.

This packet is then coded, tagged and prepared in various ways for input to the computer, which first checks it for validation, then assigns the whole packet to a place on a random access file. In return we get back a full set of rotated index entries on cards to serve as our main authority file, together with a machine-generated number which uniquely identifies that particular subject packet for future reference. From that time on, whenever the indexing team recognise that the subject they are dealing with matches a set of entries already on the file, they need only to quote this number back to the machine and it will reproduce the entire packet of data, and assign these various class numbers and headings to their correct places on the MARC record for the book in hand, with no need for further effort by the other subject teams.

It is too early yet to say just how successful this procedure will be in reducing the intellectual tasks of classing and indexing, but already, after four months' working, something like 20% of our throughput can be handled in this way, and the proportion is rising steadily as more subjects go into the system.

I realise that in this brief introduction to PRECIS I have dealt less than adequately with some of the most difficult problems in the field of subject indexing. I have tried, however, to make two particular points concerning the work we are doing in London. The first is the lesson we had to learn the hard way—that if we want to exploit the computer to its best advantage in information work we must also be prepared to revise many of our traditional approaches to the organisation of subject data. The second point arises out of this. We are beginning to get some practical results from our researches, and can show a regularly produced subject index as evidence, but there is no doubt that we still have a long way to go before we dare claim to understand this new approach to subject organisation based on whatever logic is invested in language. In view of the probable expansion of the MARC service beyond the English-speaking countries we are becoming especially interested in the possibility that an order of concepts based on the idea of context-dependency might enable us to produce meaningful subject statements in languages other than English. We have been carrying out some experiments recently in producing PRECIS versions of entries in languages such as German, Czech, Russian and Sinhalese. The results so far appear to be very encouraging, especially since we have established a relationship between the three parts of our entry structure and the changes of case in these other languages, but I would be the first to admit that we have hardly started yet to explore this linguistic route to information handling.

DISCUSSION

Dr. *Welt* asked what kind of computer storage was used for the PRECIS system and how the languages had been chosen for investigation.

Mr. *Austin* replied that a disc pack was used for this purpose and that the entire packet of subject information was identified on the file by a 'SIN' (subject index number) which identified the disc pack, the individual disc in the pack, the disc segment, the segment track, and the nearest reading head.

In relation to the experiments with different languages, these had been self-selecting, i.e. members of the BNB staff happened to speak these languages. Singhalese had presented the biggest problem because of the large number of inflections which it employed. It had been pointed out that all the languages so far used were of the Indo-Aryan group and he now wished to do some indexing in Basque, which, he had been given to understand, belonged to no discernible family of languages, and also in some of the African languages.

In response to another question Mr. Austin said that there had been no time, as yet, to investigate indexing time thoroughly. However, following the postal strike in Britain, the four indexers appointed to handle BNB's throughput of 30,000 volumes a year were indexing 190 to 200 books per day.

Mrs. *Sherwood* asked how a string of concepts which already had a subject index number was identified, i.e. whether this was done by the indexer or by the computer, and, if the former, what happened if such a string was not identified.

Mr. *Austin* replied that the indexers were supposed to identify such strings and had available, as a desk tool, an authority file of all strings so far used, which was produced by the computer and updated regularly. The situation of a failure to identify an existing string had not yet arisen. Mr. *Freeman* wondered if consideration had been given to the use of the role indicators as a device for reducing recall in the possible future use of the files for information retrieval.

Mr. *Austin* said that he hoped that in future the system would employ a string of notated elements with the role indicators included and at that time the file could be searched with or without the use of the role indicators in the search program. He drew attention to the fact that studies involving the use of role indicators had been made in "hard" vocabulary fields such as aeronautics and high-speed aerodynamics in the Cranfield studies, where, he believed, role indicators were probably unnecessary because the relationships between such terms as "wing", "drag", "swept-back" and "flow" were unambiguous. However, the restructuring of the PRECIS role indicators had been done in the course of a research project involving *Sociology of Education Abstracts:* in a field such as this with a "soft" vocabulary it was very necessary to use role indicators in order to establish the correct relationships between terms such as "teacher", "society", and "responsibility".

THE UNIVERSAL DECIMAL CLASSIFICATION AS AN INTERNATIONAL SWITCHING LANGUAGE

Geoffrey A. Lloyd

Classification Department FID
Fédération Internationale de Documentation
The Hague, Netherlands

Four questions, with special reference to the needs of the joint UNESCO/ICSU project UNISIST are examined:

- why is an international switching language essential today?
- why is the UDC advocated by the FID for this purpose?
- how can the UDC help to promote systems interconnection and compatability and to minimize interlingual and interdisciplinary barriers?
- what should be done to fit the UDC for this important role?

Little originality is claimed for this paper, which summarizes and expands material presented over the last decade or longer mainly by circles associated with the FID (Fédération Internationale de Documentation), more particularly by members of its Central Classification Committee (FID/CCC) (2, 3, 9, 10, 11, 13, 14). It even draws on some of the ideas expressed during the thirties and forties by F. Donker Duyvis, whose name should always be linked with the two Belgian pioneers Otlet and La Fontaine and the group of European enthusiasts — among them Bradford, Lancaster Jones and Pollard in Britain, and Walther and Frank in Germany — who transformed Melvil Dewey's Decimal Classification (DC, 5th ed.) into what later became known as the Classification Décimale Universelle (CDU), or to us the Universal Decimal Classification (UDC).

Why is an international switching language essential today?

The rapidly increasing production, transfer and consumption of scientific information — call it 'information explosion' if nuclear, population and drug explosions are not enough — present the scientific-technical community, and therefore our profession, with serious problems of international exchange and availability of information that can benefit by discussion in symposia such as this and the one to be held in Yugoslavia next month.*

The advent of the computer, now in the third generation within a single span of human procreation, together with other swiftly developing mechanization aids, can help us handle the sheer bulk or mass of information and data produced, but more than ever the scientists need our help to acquire, store, retrieve, analyse, disseminate and and even evaluate it, whether in traditional or in modern mechanized systems. Computers and automation as such, indeed, will not prevent the dangerous trend from subject specialization to fragmentation, nor will intercommunication, despite Telstar and the dominance of the English language, get us any nearer the information heaven than the Tower of Babel, unless we can adopt, maintain and use one standard switching language to control the currents and interconnect the lines of information flow in all their interlingual and interdisciplinary diversity.

To support this contention, let me quote some passages from Dr. Harrison Brown's Transmissal Memorandum in the report of the joint UNESCO/ICSU Central Committee to study the feasibility of a World Scientific Information System—UNISIST (14) (the italics are mine):

"It is alleged that scientific and technical articles and reports are increasing at a rate which makes it extremely difficult for scientists to keep up with the work of their colleagues. Faulty distribution practices and understocked and understaffed libraries make access to these reports difficult; once success is had, *linguistic barriers* interpose comprehension difficulties . . . Less obvious, but more radical, are the changing needs of the world scientific community for information. The *interdisciplinary approach* to problems of the environment, for example, requires information drawn from a variety of sciences: chemistry, biology, sociology, to name only a few. The emerging needs of applied science, technology and engineering add further complexities . . .

As electronic processing and retrieval systems are developed without provision for their *compatibility,* are the scientific information services constructing a Tower of Babel? Instead of improving international communication in the sciences, will they worsen it by fragmentation into thousands . . . of independent systems, each of which to some extent re-does the work of the others?"

Strong words, though no more than a cry in the wilderness if nothing is to be done! But here is Recommendation 4 (Subject specification) from the same UNISIST synopsis:

"The attention of scientists, learned societies and information science associations should be drawn to the need for joint efforts in developing better tools for the control and conversion of natural and indexing languages in science and technology. UNISIST adherents should be invited in particular to consider the initiation of a few pilot projects, under the sponsorship of scientific organizations, aimed at testing new methodological and organizational devices in this respect, with a special emphasis on international and interdisciplinary requirements."

---

* International symposium on UDC in relation to other indexing languages. Herceg Novi (Yugoslavia), June 28 to July 1, 1971.

If the UDC can hardly be considered new, it is still clearly in the running — albeit after some plastic surgery — for we read further in the explanatory note to Recommendation 4 (just quoted):

"Agreement among the information systems on definitions for the broad categories of science (i.e. the classic disciplines and the new interdisciplinary fields) would have practical benefits for the inventorying of resources as well as for referral functions, and would appear to be attainable. The use of the *Universal Decimal Classification* in particular, for this purpose, has been advocated. Its further potential has yet to be realized, and both *a continuing programme to strengthen UDC* and further studies and experiments to test its applicability to retrieval systems are desirable . . ."

Cautious, perhaps, but certainly a recognition of the 76-year-old UDC whose expectation of life, Ranganathan claims, has expired, and whose anachronistic structure the Rangan-avant-garde of faceted classification so often dismiss — to use the original French near-epitaph — as 'ce monstre préhistorique'. It is good that UNISIST, probably the most ambitious of any project of cooperation in the field of information science, sees this problem of subject specification in its international aspect as Programme objective and priority no. 1, and that the UDC — with all its shortcomings — is singled out as an important potential component of such a major information transfer chain—from the libraries, through the abstracting, indexing and translating services, to the information analysis centres; for here is one of the main information problems of today — systems interconnection, how to make full use of modern mechanization techniques, not to increase fragmentation, but to preserve and improve interlingual and interdisciplinary contacts between scientists all over the world.

Why is the UDC advocated by FID as an international switching language?

Why, then, the UDC, rather than its parent DC or the LC, or indeed Bliss' Bibliographic Classification (BC) or Ranganathan's Colon Classification (CC)—to mention only the "big five" among general classification schemes? Without wishing to underestimate the respective uses and value of these four existing giants, one cannot ignore the relative inflexibility of DC and the U.S. tendency towards reclassification, albeit by LC—despite the counterblast from Perreault (10), nor can one overlook the comparatively small usership and revision facilities of the BC and CC, which leaves only LC as a serious existing contender for the role of international switching language. But, despite the powerful appeal of its catalogue card service and the MARC format, not least in developing countries where ready-made devices like these are particularly attractive, LC can hardly compare with the UDC in the matters of international notation, depth documentation, retrieval and mechanization facilities.

Ten years ago, the Aslib Cranfield Project under Cleverdon showed that UDC compared quite well with a special (facet) scheme, with Uniterm and A/Z indexing techniques: in a recent Aslib study by Vickery and colleagues for UNISIST, the UDC was found to be 'the least unsatisfactory' of the major existing schemes; and now Mills, in the brief UDC section of a comprehensive review of progress in library classification (*J.Doc.*, 26(2), June 1970, p. 141-3) admits that UDC "has continued to adapt itself, slowly and unsteadily, but with surprising persistence, to the new demands imposed on it." Apart from these general judgments, and the UNISIST reference, there are three good reasons that can be advanced in support of the UDC:

(i) As regards *usership and availability,* the estimates from a dozen FID National Members in answer to a 1968 questionnaire (6) indicate 100,000 institutional users as a conservative estimate—mainly, it is true, in the USSR, Poland and other East European states, but there is a substantial number in Latin America and Japan, as well as in Germany and other West European countries. Although in the English-speaking world usership is still more difficult to assess, one could probably put it at about 10,000 in view of the 30,000 copies of the English full and abridged editions sold or distributed during the last 20 years.

Availability of UDC in a wide range of editions in some 20 languages, at several levels and of varied scope — full, abridged, medium-length and special-subject schedules — is obviously responsible, to a large extent, for the massive usership claimed, and could help to make UDC even more attractive to future users, provided that some very necessary organizational improvements (to be touched on later) can be made by the FID and its Central Classification Committee.

(ii) *Usability of the UDC* in modern mechanized retrieval and dissemination systems, as well as for traditional cataloguing and indexing, filing and retrieval purposes in libraries and smaller documentation centres, is of course paramount today, but this vital aspect is dealt with in the paper by Malcolm Rigby, one of the U.S. pioneers in this field. (11, 12) Suffice it here to say that his efforts, coupled with those of Freeman and Atherton (4) in the AIP-UDC project of 1965-68 and other U.S. investigators, the work of Schneider and Koch of the Zentralstelle für maschinelle Dokumentation (ZMD) in Germany, of Corbett with other U.K. Atomic Energy Authority colleagues and several others (notably in the U.S.A., Britain and Denmark) have blazed a trail for recent rather encouraging applications—for example by Hindson and his two colleagues McCash and Carmichael (7) for user profiles in the British Steel Corporation, by Doris Heaps (University of Alberta) for the Boreal Institute Library in Edmonton, Canada, and by Stüdeli of Sulzer Bros. in Switzerland. The AIP-UDC project and other pioneering projects were reported in the Proceedings of the First Seminar on UDC in a mechanized retrieval system held in Copenhagen in 1968 (FID Publ. 405, FID/CR Report no. 9), whilst reports of further applications are included in the Proceedings of the 2nd Seminar on UDC and mechanization held in Frankfurt/Main in 1970 (FID/CR Report no. 11).

(iii) *The organizational set-up of UDC* — small by comparison with DC and LC — at least consists of an international centre in the FID Secretariat in The Hague, though this sorely needs more manpower, more funds and, above all, modern management. Given these improvements and a close-knit editorial control group, with the CCC as a general policy-making and steering group, there is no reason why UDC organization should not be able, by 1975 or so, to cope effectively with the demands of an international switching language.

All this is not to belittle the efforts of members of the London Classification Research Group (CRG) and *British National Bibliography (BNB)* and other explorers seeking a new general faceted classification, such as may be emerging in the CRG/BNB-based PRECIS (described in the paper by Austin), nor the ingenious *Thesaurofacet* described by Jean Aitchison, which seems to point the way for thesaurus/classification combinations in more general information systems and networks, but these are not yet necessarily the optimum solution, and hardly offer a viable alternative as an international switching language.

How can the UDC help to promote
systems interconnection and compatibility?

The two ways in which UDC can help systems interconnection, that is by minimizing the language-barrier and the incompatibility of special-subject indexing systems, both depend on the fact that it is an artificial indexing/retrieval language, using an internationally familiar notation of almost exclusively arabic numerals, with the terms and definitions relevant to each concept scheduled in many natural languages.

First then, the UDC can provide concordances tantamount to a multilingual encyclopaedia, and so make compatible in a single major information system any number of different natural languages that may be used for input and/or output. The United States and English-speaking world generally is fortunate in its dominant mother-tongue, so widely used as a lingua franca throughout a great part of the world and in thesauri and descriptor-lists, but the importance of a neutral language may be much clearer to peoples not so familiar with English, especially to Russians, Japanese, Chinese, Arabs and others who do not use Roman characters but do use arabic numerals. Even for information systems based predominantly on the English language, there will be the problem of technical translation, and for this the UDC with its many-language schedules can also provide a valuable dictionary-type tool.

Secondly, perhaps even more usefully, the UDC could serve as an interdisciplinary reference norm for the ever-increasing numbers of thesauri available, not only for relatively narrow subjects but also in wider fields of engineering (EJC/TEST, NASA, etc.), the biomedical sciences (e.g. NLM/MeSH used for MEDLARS) and social sciences (e.g. ALD Aligned List of Descriptors, joint publication of the OECD, Organization for Economic Cooperation & Development with four other bodies), not to mention the countless special classification schemes in these and other subject-areas.

Among the several attempts made to interest important international organizations during the last few years were the FID's approach to the Council of Europe's relevant committee to support the preparation of a broad concordance between UDC and the International Classification of Patents (ICP), and to the International Organization for Standardization (ISO) Central Secretariat to use UDC in combination with its newly espoused keyword list for its central information service in Geneva—an effort which was strongly supported with a very comprehensive proposal by Wellisch (16). Neither in these two cases nor in other similar approaches, however, was there a positive response, despite declarations of agreement in principle, and it has become steadily clearer that the trend towards the use of descriptor-lists reflects often an ignorance of the advantages of hierarchic schemes with their encouragement to browse and explore related fields.

Still adhering to its policy of promoting UDC in a switching role, the FID then decided to concentrate on seeking contracts for concordances between the UDC and various descriptor lists and thesauri, such as the ALD and the EJC/TEST. Unesco, with whom FID has close relations, were developing their new Computerized Documentation Service (CDS) in 1969-70 to cover all their main subject interests and had also become interested in the ALD, in which the International Council for Social Sciences Documentation (ICSSD) played a significant role, so that it has recently been possible to secure for FID two Unesco contracts for the preparation of UDC concordances

(a) with the Unesco/CDS descriptor-list of about 2600 terms, and
(b) with two (ICSSD-prepared) descriptor lists for economics and sociology.

The work on these projects has only just begun, but initial indications are that there may be mutual benefits for both the UDC and the descriptor lists concerned. Moreover, there is room for more studies on the *combined use* of UDC and thesauri for information retrieval in various subject-fields, such as recently done for nuclear science (8).

Unfortunately, Unesco interest did not extend to the EJC/TEST — in its wide scope and extensive adoption one of the most important of any thesauri to date — so that FID/CCC decided to appoint a three-man group to carry out a pilot project, in the hope that the results would be sufficiently encouraging to submit a request to some major funding body to support financially a full-scale concordance. This three-man team is headed by Wellisch, whose encouraging report (18), based on about 180 EJC/TEST terms coded with UDC numbers, indicates that:

(a) 80-90% of TEST descriptors can be UDC-coded 'with sufficient precision to warrant accepting UDC as a highly suitable switching language for translated versions of TEST;

(b) the UDC medium editions, with a full array of auxiliaries, are almost adequate for this, so that future efforts at revision could better concentrate on these than on detailed perfection of the full editions;

(c) mutual enrichment, e.g. supplying of missing terms in UDC and better structuring of TEST, can result from well-made concordances of the type undertaken.

As the number of thesauri, keyword- and descriptor-lists multiplies, so does the need increase for more studies of switching and reconciliation devices (2, 9) but the preliminary indications from the UDC/TEST concordance already strengthen our confidence that the UDC could play a key role in this respect, i.e. as a micro-switching language between terms for the same concept in different languages or as used in different disciplines.

*What should be done to fit the UDC
for an international switching role?*

Having earlier noted the need in major information transfer systems like the projected UNISIST for a relatively broad (macro-) switching language between specific thesauri, etc., and having seen the UDC's potentiality for more detailed (meso- or micro-) switching between sections or terms of a particular thesaurus like EJC/TEST, we may ask what should be done to fit the UDC for either — or both — of these international switching roles.

Two corresponding approaches seem desirable:

(a) to set about constructing an overall UDC macro-switching code of no more than a thousand or two UDC numbers in which, at suitable switch-points or nodes, references could be listed to appropriate thesauri and/or special classifications, as well as to further detailed UDC divisions for the benefit of the many who use UDC in depth;

(b) to carry out further projects for UDC concordances with authoritative thesauri and other indexing schemes in as many subject-fields as possible, and to experiment with the problem of trying to fix optimum switch or node levels for subject-retrieval at different depths.

The idea of the UDC as a macro-switching language for central control and coordination of the peripheral units in a multilingual, multidisciplinary information retrieval systems, of the links in an information-transfer chain, has been given new impetus in FID circles by a recent proposal to compile a UDC 'roof code' with a series of 'mobile facets', each applicable beyond its own discipline: according to Arntz (1) it would have a schedule of not more than 1000-2000 numbers, though capable of elaboration to abridged-edition level (say 10-15,000 numbers) and medium-edition level (say 40-50,000 numbers), perhaps even extending in some sections to full-edition level (150-200,000). An essential feature of this 'roof code' would be to include the most urgent updatings of terminology and as much structural-notational improvement as would be acceptable without a total rebuilding — a process which would obviously take many years to complete, if indeed it could be done at all without transforming the UDC into a quite new decimal classification. Were the construction of such a new international system to be attempted in 15 or 20 years — and I would not rule it out, whether as a variant, complement or competitor to a new faceted general scheme — it would have to have a relatively limited display of the classic disciplines and a more modern array of the many interdisciplinary subject-fields recognized today, with a sufficient, but simpler, apparatus of relators, facet and role indicators. This would seem to presuppose some kind of reconciliation — if not a merger — between the DC and UDC, with a great deal more give and take on both sides than seems possible just now.

Just how drastic the minimum essential transformation of the UDC structure and notation must be has not yet been thought out by FID/CCC, but it is unlikely to go as far as the metamorphosis advocated by Inge Dahlberg (3), tempting though many of her ideas are. Presently, the most urgent need of all for the UDC, if it is to fulfil the new demands of major information systems like UNISIST, is to have the whole organizational set-up on a sounder basis: this will need the application of modern management techniques and equipment in the central office, extending beyond the automatic tape-typewriting machine recently installed, and a four- or five-man editorial team to handle the technical updating and revision work centrally, leaving the 25-man FID/CCC to play a very necessary policy-making and consultative role rather than concern itself with actual schedule-making. This proposal has been advanced and elaborated in a recent article by Wellisch (17), but takes us beyond the purpose and limits of this paper, which were to summarize current trends and future prospects for the development of the UDC as an international switching language.

REFERENCES

1. ARNTZ, H. "Die DK - eine Vielfacettenklassifikation". [The UDC—a many-faceted classification.] *Nachr. Dok.* v. 21, no. 4, Aug. 1970, p. 139-142.

2. COATES, E.J. "Switching Languages for Indexing". *J. Doc.*, v. 26, no. 2, June 1970, p. 102-110.

3. DAHLBERG, I. "Möglichkeiten einer Neugestaltung der DK". [Possibilities for a renewal of UDC.] *Nachr. Dok.*, v. 21, no. 4, Aug. 1970, p. 141-153.

4. FREEMAN, R.R. "'Actual and Potential Role of the Universal Decimal Classification in Language-sciences Documentation". *In: Proc. Conf. held at Airlie House* March 4-6, 1966, under the sponsorship of the Center for Applied Linguistics. New York, American Elsevier, 1968, p. 8.

5. LLOYD, G.A. "A 'New Deal' for Universal Classification". *Rev. Doc.*, v. 27, no. 2, May 1960, p. 149-153.

6. LLOYD, G.A. "The UDC in its International Aspects". *Aslib Proc.*, v. 21, no. 5, May 1969, p. 204.

7. McCASH, W.H. and CARMICHAEL, J.J. "UDC User Profiles as Developed for a Computer-based SDI Service in the Iron and Steel Industry". *J. Doc.*, v. 26, no. 4, Dec. 1970, p. 295-312.

8. MAROSI, A. "EURATOM Thesaurus and UDC: Combined Use for the Subject Organization of a Small Information Service". *J. Doc.*, v. 25, no. 3, Sept. 1969, p. 197-213.

9. NEVILLE, H.H. "Feasibility Study of a Scheme for Reconciling Thesauri Covering a Common Subject". *J. Doc.*, v. 26, no. 4, Dec. 1970, p. 313-336.

10. PERREAULT, J.M. "UDC and Reclassification". Ch. 15, 16, 17 *in: Towards a Theory for UDC*. London, Bingley, 1970. p. 183-241.

11. RIGBY, M. "Standardization for Classification in Computerized Documentation Systems". *In:* P. Atherton (ed.) *Classification Research: Proc. 2nd International Study Conference, Elsinore 1964*. Copenhagen, Munksgaard 1965. (FID 370). p. 524-538.

12. RIGBY, M. "A Mechanized Multi-access Documentation System for the Atmospheric Sciences and Water Resources". *In: Proc. 2nd Annual American Water Resources Conference 1965*. Urbana, Ill. 1967. p. 415-431.

13. SVIRIDOV, F. A. and G. A. LLOYD. "Medical Documentation and the UDC". *In: Proc. 3rd International Congress of Medical Librarianship,* Amsterdam, 5-9 May 1969. Amsterdam, Excerpta Medica. (International congress series no. 208)

14. *UNISIST: Synopsis of the Feasibility Study on a World Science Information System by the U.N. Educational, Scientific & Cultural Organization (UNESCO) and the International Council of Scientific Unions (ICSU).* Paris, Unesco, 1971.

15. U.S. NATIONAL BUREAU OF STANDARDS. *Cooperation, Convertibility and Compatibility among Information Systems: a Literature Review.* Washington, 1966. (*Its* Miscellaneous publication 276). Especially p. 75-77 and 98-99.

16. WELLISCH, H. *An International Centre for Standards Documentation.* Tel Aviv, Israel Society of Special Libraries and Information Centres, 1969. (Contributions to Information Science no. 3)

17. WELLISCH, H. "Organisatorische Neuordnung des DK-Systems." [Organizational renewal of the UDC system.] *Nachrichten für Dokumentation,* v. 22, no. 2, April 1971, p. 55-63.

18. WELLISCH, H. "A Concordance between UDC and TEST (Thesaurus of Engineering and Scientific Terms); Results of a Pilot Project." *In: Proc. International Symposium on UDC in Relation to Other Indexing Languages,* Herceg Novi (Yugoslavia), 1971. (In press.)

DISCUSSION

M. *de Grolier* asked what exactly Mr. Lloyd meant by the term "switching language".

Mr. *Lloyd* replied that he had two things in mind when using the term: firstly, UDC could be a kind of "roof" code of not more than a few thousand headings. This would be a kind of concordance to available special thesauri and classification schemes under UDC numbers. Secondly, he envisaged a more detailed kind of concordance, such as that being made by Wellisch and his colleagues. Again, if individual users wished to go beyond the level of a "middle edition" of UDC they would either have to arrange for the publication of special subject editions or produce their own special schemes. He believed that there was no longer any possibility for managing at one center like the FID, or anywhere else, the enormous "pre-historic monster" known as the full edition of UDC.

Mr. *Welt* noted that in an explosive field, such as that referred to by Mr. Rigby, the high-productivity period was of relatively short duration and he wished to know whether FID could act swiftly enough to get terms into use before productivity declined again.

Mr. *Lloyd* doubted whether such immediate action was necessary since one could, in a hierarchical system, either class a new topic at the broader head, or allocate it to a special "new concept" number temporarily. Of course, one would have to reclassify subsequently.

Mr. *Freeman* commented that FID was a model of democracy, giving representation to subject specialists and to national groups and this was not particularly conducive to speedy operation.

THE UDC IN MECHANIZED SUBJECT
INFORMATION RETRIEVAL

Malcolm Rigby

National Oceanic and Atmospheric Agency,
Scientific Information and Documentation Division,
Rockville, Maryland

Introduction

We have for some time been acutely aware of the wide variety of subject retrieval systems or modes available to an information systems designer. Now we are certain that a special system is available or may be adapted to suit any given collection, situation or purpose.

In this discussion, the criteria for choice or development of a system or systems for subject indexing, retrieval or browsing will first be examined from a theoretical and a practical point of view. Next the relative merits and limitations of the UDC for certain types and sizes of collection will be argued. Finally the use of the UDC in mechanized information or data retrieval systems and the use of automatic data processing equipment for maintaining and improving the UDC by itself and in concordance with other subject indexing systems will be touched upon.

The fact should be kept in mind that, whereas the UDC is actually universal in the sense that it covers all branches of knowledge, in practice it has from the start been a controlled collection of special hierarchical systems with a unifying notation structure and coordination mechanism. Although it is universal in the sense of being independent of language or orthography, yet it is hospitable to various languages and alphabets. Whereas it is itself a programming language, it requires special instructions as to filing, sorting and display in either a manual or a machine mode. Finally, whereas it has greater versatility than almost any other subject indexing or classification system, it is most often used, or misused, for purposes other than those for which it was originally intended (such as linear shelving or vocabulary control). It has therefore aroused considerable dissatisfaction among the users who want a perfect system for their peculiar uses, and controversy among those who are charged with developing and maintaining the system (for instance whether to subdivide hierarchically as originally intended or to subdivide by coordination or use of special auxiliaries in a permutable or even a non-permutable fashion).

The UDC, then, is basically an hierarchical classification system which may be used, if care is taken, for indexing (rather than shelving) documents or articles (rather than books) in some depth, without regard for language or alphabet, and to any desired degree of generality or specificity. It can also, by means of auxiliaries, take cognizance of universal facets such as time, place, form, language, point of view, and many special facets peculiar to separate branches of knowledge. Other uses are permissible but should not be allowed to alter or corrupt the basic system.

Criteria for Choice

Retrieval of documents for their subject content, in contrast to retrieval by author or institution or project or country or language, is highly subjective and cannot ever approach perfection, but can only be more or less effective, more or less complete, or more or less precise.

What is judged to be better or worse, then, depends as much on the objectives or habits of the searcher as on the system or what is in the system. In any event, whether searching is done by the user, by an intermediary or by a machine (or man-machine combination), browsing is almost inevitably the last stage (if not the first stage) of the search. It would be highly unlikely that a subject search would turn up, on the first go-around, the one and only (or the ten and only) book or document relevant to the searcher's needs, although the likelihood of his being satisfied with the one (or ten) document retrieved, as a starting point or even as the ad hoc answer to his immediate needs, is far greater. In fact he might be better satisfied with a few relevant documents from the much larger population of relevant material, than with *all possible* relevant documents by his or anyone's criteria. The gap between *an* answer and *the* answer, therefore, may be very great and hence evaluation of effectiveness almost impossible.

So the problem faced in setting up or in modifying a subject retrieval system is not how to develop the *perfect* system, but how to make the location of relevant material by browsing less cumbersome or uncertain than would be possible in a randomly-arranged collection of books or documents.

Size of Collection

The system or systems chosen for making browsing by man or machine less onerous (or more effective) depends largely on the size and the nature of the collection. For each increase of an order of magnitude in the number of documents or books or references, a new approach must be considered, and for different special subjects or purposes some modifications are required. Furthermore, a system which will best suit the whole universe of subjects, or cultures, or languages, or types of publication, or periods of history, may not be the most suitable for any one of the special aspects or situations. A system best suited for shelving (linear arrangement) or for depth retrieval, may not be valid for co-ordinate indexing; and one suitable for literature may not be the best for geography or chemistry or medicine.

For the sake of discussion, a rough "model" might be employed, but allowance must be made for variations from the "average" owing to the varying character and complexity of collections, or of users' habits and requirements.

The scale used, like the Richter Earthquake Magnitude Scale, is exponential, i.e. each additional class or unit is an order-of-magnitude greater than the previous one. Recognition is made of the "square-root law" for the number of guide cards in a library catalog (Ben-Ami Lipetz) (19) as being along analogous lines of thinking.

A final observation: *if a collection is large enough and varied enough to require the use of machines, its vocabulary will be large and varied enough to require some sort of structuring, or on the other hand if a structured (classified) system is indicated, an alphabetical approach (index) should be provided to allow direct access to the classification system, to permit choice of alternative hierarchies, if they exist, and to take over where memory fails. Ideally the user should have a choice of approaches depending on habits and circumstances of each search, and this is the essence of the interactive mode.*

Table 1
SIZE OF COLLECTION VS. SUBJECT RETRIEVAL APPROACH

Scale No.	Log Scale	Number of Documents (average)	Number of Subject Classes	Terms	Type of System	Examples of Collection
1	10	50	5(1/10)	5(1/10)	Random	Office-desk
2	10^2	500	25(1/20)	50(1/10)	Browsing	Home Library
3	10^3	5,000	125(1/40)	500(1/10)	Mnemonic	Departmental Library
4	10^4	50,000	625(1/80)	5,000(1/10)	Abridged Control	Special Library
5	10^5	500,000	3,125(1/160)	50,000(1/10)	Detailed Control	Major Public or Govt. Lib.
6	10^6	5,000,000	15,625(1/320)	500,000(1/10)	Multi-Access	University Library
7	10^7	50,000,000	78,125(1/640)	5,000,000(1/10)	Complex Universal	Worldwide System
8	10^8	500,000,000	400,000(1/1280)	50,000,000(1/10)	Ultimate	Possible Universe

We all know that the eye can scan a dozen or so books, no matter in what order, and select a book on a given subject with considerable success, in about 10 seconds. But if the collection grows to 100-1000 books (or documents or citations), some subject arrangement is required if one is to have equal success in less than a minute of searching. The obvious solution is to arrange by some arbitrary grouping of titles of like subject content at first (say 10 general subject areas) with later subdivision as the collection reaches 500 (50 mnemonically arranged groups). From 1,000-10,000 a more professionally developed scheme must be used; from 10,000 to 100,000 some authoritative scheme (either a class scheme with A/Z index, or an alphabetic scheme with class control, or a thesaurus, or coordinate scheme) is a must, and from 100,000 to 1,000,000 a dual system with both direct and indirect access is essential to efficient location.

Above class 6 (1 million) every rational mode of access must be considered, the best electronic devices to coordinate the most detailed class or descriptor (or both) subject indicators so that 100,000 to 500,000 terms can, by permutation, yield 5,000,000 or more compound or complex indicators which is required for a universe of 50 to 100 million records if one is to maintain a search capability for browsing through 5-50 (average 10) titles in less than a minute (as with class 1 or 2 systems).

Suggested Systems for Classes of Collections
Class one (10-100)

No retrieval system, arrange in the most suitable manner for occasion by size, color, crude subject association or according to special interests—no index needed, no vocabulary needed—retrieval by eye and memory.

Class two (100-1,000)

Author catalog useful, shelving labels would help in browsing—logical arrangement with some sub-arrangement (or association) assists in quick scanning, whether on shelves or in files of cards or on sheets. Keysort cards might be helpful. Simple index (on cards or sheets) easily prepared and time-saving. No need to coordinate with other collections or systems. Memory is sufficient.

Class three (1,000-10,000)

Here one cannot rely any longer on memory either for location or vocabulary, but must have a well-tried system or else develop one with great care and foresight.

The unit-term or simple coordinate or controlled vocabulary systems are quite sufficient in most cases, for a vocabulary of 500 terms, or a class system of 400-500 categories would yield 5-15 items or documents per heading or class—ideal for browsing. By all means be sure that the collection is not going to continue to grow beyond the 10,000 threshold before buying a closed system.

The time to start planning for the most effective system or systems comes when:

Size: The collection passes the 1,000 mark, shows signs of steady or accelerated growth, and appears to be of permanent value or status.

Vocabulary: The subject matter shows signs of expanding into new or borderline fields—i.e. the vocabulary is growing explosively or requests becoming more specific.

Products: There is a need for periodic and cumulative indexes or announcements, as well as arrangement.

Machines: The use of electronic or even simple machines is contemplated.

Thus the criteria for selection should be those of the *next* order of magnitude — when passing the 10,000 mark after one or two years, plan for 10-100 years, i.e. a system in the 100,000-1,000,000 class — (the 1,000,000-10,000,000 class system might be too costly and cumbersome, and would not be required for over a century, at which time systems may be completely unrecognizable by today's lights).

Class four (10,000-100,000)

If the collection is never going above 50,000-100,000 records or documents, because of self-weeding, space, short half-life, slow growth or a closed subject-field, a single-access system is probably sufficient.

This may take one or another of several forms, with a vocabulary of 1,000 or 2,000 terms or categories:

1) *Shelving* according to any standard system such as DC, LC, UDC (abridged) or by accession number (with a subject index).
2) *Indexing* by:
   a) *Controlled subject headings* from any authority list or one made for the occasion.
   b) *KWIC Indexes* at annual or semi-annual intervals.
   c) *Coordinate indexes* if the subject-field is homogeneous.
3) *Retrieval* by Thesaurus if mechanized.

If the collection is going to grow beyond the 100,000 level in 5-15 years (or less), then the criteria and systems for the next class should be considered (i.e. 100,000-1,000,000).

Most special libraries in government agencies, public libraries in big cities, abstracting and indexing services in major disciplines or missions, and many industrial libraries are in this ball-park, and may have passed the million mark after 10 or 15 years of cumulative growth.

Class five (100,000-1,000,000)

To browse through a file of 500,000 records one must have the capability of narrowing the search down to 5-50 items, by some means or other, in a few minutes.

This requires either:

1) Access by *detailed* (and that means quite open-ended) *subject headings* (an average of 20,000-30,000 terms).

2) Access by *detailed* (possibly strictly controlled but also open-ended) *classification system* (average 10,000-15,000 faceted categories).

3) Access by *coordination of detailed terms or categories* either pre-coordinated terms to 2 or 3 or even 4 words each, or 4-8 digit class codes. For example rather than coordinate A:B:H:K:N:P:S:X:Z requiring 9 coordinating operations, with a high probability that any one would be missing and so a *no hit* is retrieved, one could coordinate (ABH) (KN) (PS) (XZ) requiring only 4 coordinating operations or even (ABHKN) (PS) (XZ) requiring only three selections and coordinations.

Some might use a verbal system internally, with retrieval by a classed system, or vice-versa—i.e. use the classed system only for shelving or for file maintenance and use natural language for queries.

The probability is very great that a system which has reached over half a million will go over a million, in which case a combination of 2 or all 3 of the above is *required,* and all 3 modes should be available to the user.

Class six (1-10 million)

This embraces most large State and University Libraries, the *major* abstracting and indexing Services (CA, BA, EI) and a few of the largest government libraries (National Agricultural Library, National Library of Medicine, Science Museum Library, etc.) and Document Systems (DDC, NTIS, NASA).

Here there has been the most hindsight, painful reappraisal of systems and excusable blundering (the economic factor *always* determines the system which will *always* be too restrictive for the traffic and too costly or time-consuming to remedy).

Here one must use every mode of access, manual and machine available. No closed or controlled system can possibly work without supplementary open-ended or even uncontrolled access modes.

If one examines the systems which are the *least objectionable,* one finds in most cases an open-ended natural language or verbal system with a vocabulary of 100,000-500,000 or more terms (controlled only for synonomy and never using anything but the most specific available term) along with a classed system of 100,000-300,000 specific headings or the capability of subdividing to that degree of specificity.

Class seven (10-100 million)

This includes the Library of Congress or the British Museum or VINITI or CNRS or the total journal literature of the century.

The vocabulary equals the total technical vocabulary (English Unabridged plus all of the special vocabularies) which amounts to over a million terms. The class scheme would approach 500,000 classes, which could be faceted to make several million classes.

The examples such as the Library of Congress or VINITI unfortunately did not plan for over 100 million records so can only be controlled by dividing the universe into a dozen or more sub-systems which would be more manageable—e.g. books and monographs separate from maps or films or manuscripts or serials, or into major subject categories such as Science and Technology or Humanities or Fine arts.

No such general system could possibly work without experts from all fields constantly improving an open ended multi-access system and many special sub-systems. This is the situation which faces UNISIST or any other worldwide general network. Class eight (>100 million) is not ridiculous when considering the entire universe of published literature and data which is retrievable by subject. Many data banks contain over 100 million discrete records, which must be subdivided by some 10 million or more *possible* categories or combinations of categories to be manageable.

The Universal Decimal Classification System in the 1970's

As mentioned above, one or other of any number of general or special systems will work for Class 3 collections or for Class 4 if static or homogeneous. But for growing or heterogeneous Class 4 (at least above 50,000 documents) or Class 5 (100,000-1,000,000) or bigger systems, a few characteristics emerge as absolutely essential to efficient and effective subject retrieval. If a network or system of libraries or services is contemplated, the problem is even more acute and complex.

1) Specificity (one cannot anticipate the degree of detail to be retrieved)
2) Generality (one must be able to broaden searches)
3) Coordinate capability (random combinations or cross-reference specifications)
4) Facet ability (for logical coordination)
5) Stability (for continuity, predictability and consistency in a cumulative data base and among sub-systems)
6) Open-endedness (for explosively developing or new fields)
7) Conciseness of notation (for economy of operation)
8) Universality of subject and scope
9) Availability—no good unless schedules may be obtained readily
10) Mechanism for updating and translating

11) Machinability—no major system will work unless machinable
12) Simplicity relative to task required
13) Logical or mnemonic structure

In spite of all of its weaknesses, many of which are due to the system being used (or misused) for purposes for which it was not intended (such as shelving books or control of vocabularies), the UDC is the only system known which has all of the above attributes. As the Soviets, French, British, German and Scandinavians have testified, the UDC is not a good system but it is the least objectionable of any universal system which could be found or developed in the coming decade or two. Furthermore it would cost millions of dollars to develop a new universal system which would be as good, and to get it accepted and in use. (1,2,3,4)

Finally with the present mechanisms for updating and translating the UDC, an acceptable system could be achieved in half of the time and for one-tenth the cost, if the money and effort were expended on the UDC.

A decade of demonstrations (5,6,7,8,9) have shown that:

1) The UDC is machinable, both for control of schedules and for retrieval or listing.

In spite of its many advantages there are a number of objections to its use. Some of these objections are valid and arise from mutually-exclusive attributes. Other objections are equally valid but the weaknesses which give rise to the criticism can be easily remedied. Finally, there are objections based on ignorance of the system or its proper uses or of the capabilities of modern automated data processing equipment.

Some of the more general objections are on account of:

1) Obsolescence in general or in many specific fields
2) Too rapid or too many changes of a radical nature
3) Complexity—too many special auxiliaries
4) Simplicity—not enough specific relators to prevent ambiguity
5) Length of groups of numbers too variable for automation
6) Groups of numbers too long for labelling, remembering or recognition
7) Too little known or used (in U.S.A.)
8) Complete schedules not available
9) Schedules too detailed for normal use
10) Schedules not detailed enough for current literature
11) No fixed order for citation—too little consistency in practice
12) No central authority which maintains the system as a whole on a consistent or rational basis
13) No single place where a given subject is classified in many instances

First, the contest between stability and responsiveness is inherent in all controlled systems, whether classed schedules or natural language or thesauri. A vocabulary-based system is more easily updated than a classed or hierarchical system, and one with a single control mechanism (one person or a local committee) more responsive than one with a complicated committee structure. Furthermore, a universal system, involving many disciplines and many languages is even harder to revise — hence more stable — than one involving a specialty in one language. Finally the notational structure imposes some constraint—once all ten "rooms" are filled it is difficult to rearrange or add new concepts at that level.

The solution to the above problem — that of minimizing delay in revision where necessary — lies in four main fields of effort: 1) organization, 2) money, 3) experts and 4) guidelines. The FID has been trying for a decade to provide better organization, more money, more active committees and to cut down time for each go-around in developing new schedules by automation and by reducing time required for acceptance or rejection of proposals.

Certainly increasing mechanization will speed up the whole revision procedure, but it will also increase demands for revision—much to the consternation of advocates of stability who count the cost and trouble involved in radical changes (as in shelving).

Second, the tension between simplicity and complexity is inherent in all systems—many want fewer headings (or descriptors) so greater numbers of references can be obtained for a given query, and so lists of terms are shorter, more easily controlled and more stable. But this puts a greater burden on the user who must browse through longer and longer lists of mostly irrelevant material to find pertinent items.

In mechanized systems, the principle that one can always *combine* discrete concepts or categories if the discrimination is made at source, but cannot discriminate if assignments are too general, is a valid and useful guide to subject analysis as well as to systems development. Therefore the system should allow the greatest possible specificity, but with the built-in ability to combine, coordinate or generalize hierarchically or otherwise, ad lib.

If you want a tool which can do complicated tasks, you need a somewhat more complicated tool than for simple or crude tasks. To express complicated ideas one needs a sophisticated language or else an evolved grammar or notation capable of linking simple terms in a variety of unambiguous sentences or formulae. The UDC has about the simplest possible structure for both specific or general expression and involved combination or coordination of concepts one could devise.

Thirdly the *length of groups* of numbers is a drawback for labelling (in shelving) books, but abridgment of long UDC numbers, or substitution of letters for basic numbers in special collections, or a combination of the two, can effectively alleviate this objection. However, the shelving of books is not the primary function of the UDC, which has been developed for documentation or bibliographic purposes for which other systems are *not* suitable.

The objection in automation is that the *variable length* of groups precludes the use of fixed-fields on punched cards for subject specification. This is no more of a problem with modern approaches to tape input (or even multiple card input) to computers than is the variable length of authors, corporate authors, serials or subject-headings, or the use of multiple subject headings. Paper is cheap and computers unbelievably fast, so this objection is becoming less relevant rather than more so.

The usual division of long UDC numbers into triads gives a rhythm to the series which has as great mnemonic value as does the use of letters, especially non-mnemonic letters, to break up or shorten the series. In practice, LC numbers may be just as long or even longer than UDC numbers to express the same degree of detail. For instance, Meteorology is QC 851-999 in LC, and 551.5 in UDC or DC, and Heating and ventilating of buildings is TH 7135 in LC, and 697 in UDC.

Fourthly, the unavailability of UDC in the U.S. and the resulting lack of knowledge about it is an historical rather than an inherent weakness. For ten years, real efforts have been made, and these efforts will pay off in the future, to insure that the UDC is taught in library schools, and more important that schedules and guides and teaching aids will be available in English as they are already in German, Spanish, Russian, Czech, Hungarian, Japanese, Dutch, etc.

The "gentleman's agreement" that UDC would not be "imported" into the U.S.A. is largely responsible for lack of knowledge, use and teaching UDC here. This loss of a major market for schedules has prevented rapid issuance of new or full schedules in English. Recognition of the fact that UDC and Dewey (or LC) each have their primary uses for bibliography, public libraries and university libraries (or special library shelving) respectively, and that classification vs. thesaurus or natural language retrieval, not conflict between classification systems, is the real battleground, is gradually gaining ground.

Next, the problem of too much or too little detail is a universal one— and it is easily solved by having two, three or four editions with varying degrees of abridgment, as is the case with UDC but not with Dewey, LC or TEST.

In many languages (at least 10 of the 15) the UDC has both abridged and full editions. The abridged averages 15-20,000 terms or an equivalent to the edition of Dewey, whereas the Full editions would run to 100-150,000 terms.

The English, French, German, Polish, Russian, Czech, Hungarian, Spanish, Portuguese and Japanese have both levels in varying stages of completion and recency.

Three languages have Intermediate editions (40-50,000 terms) in one volume (or a second for alphabetical index), the French, German and Russian, and an English Intermediate Edition is forthcoming.

Several languages have even smaller abridged editions (3,000-5,000 terms) for small collections.

Special editions have come out in the major languages to take care of the universal problem wanting greater specificity in *core* areas and specificity (or fewer terms) in related or distantly related disciplines— hence, a profile of interest edition for Education, Nuclear Science, Metallurgy, Geology, etc.

Finally, single vs. multiple location is also a universal problem that stems from:

1) Ambiguity of terminology
2) Multiple hierarchies
3) Natural tendency to take in more territory than is warranted.

The UDC is less subject to criticism and less cumbersome than natural language systems (or LC) in the first regard.

Summary and Conclusions

Over the next decade or two the number, size and complexity of information systems is going to increase immeasurably all over the world. At present there are a dozen types of subject retrieval systems and scores or even hundreds of variations or combinations thereof. We predict that there will be an even greater variety of local retrieval systems but for that very reason there will be a growing need for one or several unifying systems or languages.

Two basic types of retrieval systems are recognized—the inductive and the deductive, or the *direct* (verbal and specific) and *indirect* classification system (usually coded). The English language subject heading, sometimes in the form of a thesaurus (which has some of the characteristics of a classification system) is the nearest one can hope to come to a unifying language for direct access to information in science and technology. For indirect access across the board, the UDC has proven in test after test to be the least objectionable, most versatile for manual and machine files, and the most generally viable as well as available in many languages and countries.

Much preparatory work has been done in the past decade to demonstrate the merits and the limitations of the UDC for computerized subject files, and to determine costs and technical problems in programming or display. It has been proven without any doubt in a dozen countries that the UDC is machinable both for indexing and for on-line retrieval, and that computers can be used to assist in maintaining and publishing UDC schedules.

Predicting the state of the art ten years from now, in such a rapidly developing field as Information Science, or in any field, can be a dangerous business. Even predicting trends over a decade or two is hazardous. However, the benefits to be derived from a distant perspective far exceed the dangers even if only a little skill can be shown (over and above a random guess or straight line extrapolation). So our crystal ball says that:

1) Demands for information are going to increase at a far more alarming rate than will the supply, either on a current (annual) basis or on a cumulative basis.

2) High speed processing, communicating and display equipment for handling bibliographic information or data are already more than adequate for the requirements of the next decade.

3) Value of data to be exchanged or re-used far exceeds the cost of collection, processing, storage, retrieval, dissemination or display— in other words, economic benefits make the costs ridiculously low.

4) Closing the gap between capability and performance, which lies in creating and maintaining the *software* and systems (such as thesauri and the UDC) *is* expensive but not when the repetitive use and universal similarities of the files and uses are considered.

5) No other Universal System equal to the UDC can possibly be developed, accepted, and made available for 10 or 15 years.

6) Hence augmented efforts will go into evolutionary (where satisfactory) and revolutionary (where unsatisfactory) revisions of the UDC for the benefit of those who do want a universal classed system. Meantime other more specialized (both by language and subject field) systems will emerge and some will be widely, but none universally, used for all fields.

7) Computerized information systems will demand improvement in both the UDC and in many language vocabularies, but computers will also greatly facilitate the revision and availability, from a psychological (added interest), from a technological (speed) and from an economic (necessity) point-of-view.

8) Finally, intellectual effort and efficient organization, not technical capabilities, are *most* necessary and it is in the very places such as this (a modern library school) that the solution will be found.

APPENDIX I
EXPERIMENTAL AND OPERATIONAL SYSTEMS

Key to abbreviations

AGI	American Geological Institute
AIP	American Institute of Physics
AUDACIOUS	Automatic Direct Access to Information with the On-line UDC System
AUWE	Admiralty Underwater Weapons Establishment
AWRE	Atomic Weapons Research Establishment
CIINTE	Centralny Instytut Informacji Naukowo-Technicznej i Ekonomicznej
DK	Dezimalklassifikation
DNA	Deutscher Normenausschuss
ESSA	Environmental Science Services Administration
FID	Fédération Internationale de Documentation
GIBUS	Groupe informatiste de bibliothèques universitaires et spécialisées
ICAS	Interdepartmental Committee on Atmospheric Sciences
M&GA	Meteorological and Geoastrophysical Abstracts
NODC	National Oceanographic Data Center
UNESCO	United Nations Educational, Scientific and Cultural Organization
UNIDEK	(a program using UDC to generate an index to articles)
WMO	World Meteorological Organization
ZMD	Zentralstelle für maschinelle Dokumentation

Canada
Computerized UDC Special Library - Boreal Institute, Univ. of Alberta (Heaps, 1969-)

Denmark
Abridged Building Classification Schedules (Fink, 1963)
UDC-Based Library Catalog (Barnholdt, 1967-)

France
GIBUS
Bibliothèque des Halles, Paris (Beyssac, 1970-)

Germany (Federal Republic)
Deutsches Hydrographisches Institut, Hamburg (Model, 1962-)
German National Bibliography (ZMD, 1966-)
Documentatio Geographica (Meynen, 1966-)
DK-Handausgabe - A/Z Index (DNA, 1967)

Israel
  Computer-Produced Regional Bibliography Eastern Mediterranean, Suez Canal and Red Sea. (Sea Fisheries Research Station, Haifa. 1969)

Italy
  Legal Mechanized Retrieval Experiments (Milan University, 1962-)

Netherlands
  ILACS (Integrated Library Administration and Cataloguing System (Dreese)

Poland
  Polish Index to Scientific Publication (CIINTE, 1968-)

Switzerland
  Sulzer Literature Dissemination and Classification (SULIC) System 1967-)

United Kingdom
  Alphabetical Subject Index to the UDC (AWRE, 1962-)
  Aldermaston Mechanical Cataloging and Ordering System (AWRE, 1962-)
  AUWE Scientific and Technical Information Center (Proposed). (1967-8)
  British Steel Corporation - Edinburgh (Colville's Computerization Project) (Hindson, 1969-)

United States of America
  Concordance Between Subject Headings and UDC - (*M&GA,* 1960-67)
  Meteorological and Geoastrophysical Titles - UNIDEK - (1961-4)
  Mechanization of UDC Schedules - Single Language - (1962-4)
  Mechanization of UDC Schedules - Multilingual - (1962-4)
  Multi-Access Indexing of Abstracts - *M&GA* - (1962-3)
  Geo-Sciences Abstracts - AGI - (1964-7)
  NODC - Automatic Selection and Indexing - (1964)
  NODC Quarterly Accessions - (1966-8)
  AIP/UDC Project - Freeman-Atherton - (1965-8)
  ICAS Vocabulary - (1965-6)
  AUDACIOUS - On-Line Retrieval - (1966-7)
  ESSA Library Holdings in Oceanography - (1968-9)
  Oceanic Index - (Mission Bay Research Foundation, 1968-9)
  Bibliography and Index of Geology - AGI - (1969-70)

International
  WMO-UDC Guide - (1967-71)
  WMO-UNESCO International Glossary of Hydrology (1969-70)
  FID - Mechanization of Schedules, P-Notes, etc. (1970-)

APPENDIX II
UDC EDITIONS IN VARIOUS LANGUAGES

The publication program of FID and its National Members provides a full range of editions on various levels and in 22 different languages.

Full editions, containing approximately 200,000 subdivisions, and issued in separate volumes, each covering one or more main classes.

Medium editions, containing some 30% of the full schedules.

Abridged editions, containing 10-15% of the full schedules.

As of 1971, the following editions are available (+) or in preparation (o):

	abridged	medium	full [1]
Arabic	o		
Czech			+
Dutch	+		
English	+	o	+ (to be completed in 1972)
Finnish	+		
French	+	+	
German	+	+	+ (complete)
Hebrew	+		
Hungarian	+		+
Italian	+		
Japanese	+		+
Macedonian	+	o	
Polish	+	o	+
Portuguese	+	o	+
Romanian			o
Russian		+	+
Serbo-Croat	+	o	o
Slovene	+	o	
Spanish	+	o	+
Swedish [2]	+		

[1] Except where indicated, not all classes have yet been published
[2] with Danish-Norwegian-Swedish index

Moreover, there are *special subject editions* containing full tables for the subject treated and other classes at abridged level. In case there is no special-subject edition, a user may select an abridged or medium edition for all classes and the relevant volumes of a full edition for subjects of interest — thus making his own special edition.

Nearly all UDC editions contain extensive alphabetical subject indexes which facilitate location of particular topics under relevant UDC numbers.

English language editions of the UDC are published in the U.K. by the British Standards Institution as their B.S. 1000. In the U.S., these editions are available from the American National Standards Institute, New York.

More information and details about the UDC editions may be found in the *Catalogue of FID Publications,* available free of charge from FID, Hofweg 7, The Hague, Netherlands.

REFERENCES

1. BARNHOLDT, B. *A Computer Based System for Production of a UDC-Classed Library Catalog at the Technological University Library of Denmark.* Danmarks Tekniske Bibliotek, Copenhagen. 1968.

2. CORBETT, L. *Report on the FID Seminar on UDC in a Mechanized Retrieval System Held at the Danish Technical University, Copenhagen. 2-6 September 1968.* AWRE Library Information Note No. 68/9, UKAEA, Aldermaston, 1968.

3. FREEMAN, R.R. "Computers and Classification Systems." *Journal of Documentation,* v. 20, no. 3, 1964. p. 137-145.

4. FREEMAN, R.R., and ATHERTON, P. *AUDACIOUS—An Experiment with an On-Line, Interactive Reference Retrieval System Using the UDC as the Index Language in the Field of Nuclear Science.* New York, American Institute of Physics, 1968. (Report AIP/UDC-7)

5. FREEMAN, R.R., and ATHERTON, P. *Final Report of the Research Project for the Evaluation of the UDC as the Indexing Language for a Mechanized Reference Retrieval System.* New York, American Institute of Physics, 1968. (Report AIP/UDC-9)

6. KOCH, K.H. *Internationale Dezimalklassifikation (DK) und elektronische Datenverarbeitung.* Frankfurt, ZMD, 1967. 67 p. (ZMD A-14)

7. RIGBY, M. *Mechanization of the UDC. Final Report on Pilot Project to Further Explore Possibilities for Mechanization of UDC Schedules.* Washington, American Meteorological Society, 1964.

8. RIGBY, M. "Experiments in Mechanized Control of Meteorological and Geoastrophysical Literature and the UDC Schedules in these Fields." *Revue Internationale de la Documentation,* v. 31, no. 3, 1964. p. 103-106. (German version: *DK-Mitteilungen,* v. 10, no. 5, 1965.)

9. RIGBY, M. "A Mechanized Multi-Access Documentation System for the Atmospheric Sciences and Water Resources." *In: Proceedings of the Second Annual American Water Resources Conference,* 1966. Urbana, Ill. 1967. p. 415-431.

10. RIGBY, M. "A World-Wide Meso-Documentation System for Collection, Storage, Retrieval and Dissemination of Water Literature." *In: International Conference on Water for Peace.* Washington, Govt. Print. Off., 1969. p. 542-555.

11. RUSSELL, M. and FREEMAN, R.R. *Computer Aided Indexing of a Scientific Abstracts Journal by the UDC with UNIDEK: a Case Study.* New York, American Institute of Physics, 1967. (Report No. AIP/UDC-4)

12. SCHNEIDER, K. und KOCH, K.H. *Verwendung von DK-Zahlen für maschinelle Registerherstellung und Information Retrieval.* Frankfurt, ZMD, 1967. (ZMD-A-10) (English version, see no. 18)

13. U.S. INTERDEPARTMENTAL COMMITTEE FOR ATMOSPHERIC SCIENCES (ICAS). *Vocabulary* (Preliminary Edition). Washington, 1966.

14. BECKER, A. M. (Sulzer Bros. Ltd., Switzerland) "Documentation and Electronic Data Processing." *American Documentation,* v. 19, no. 3, 1968. p. 311-316.

15. GALLIZIA, A; MARETTI, E. and MOLLAME, F. (Center for Documentation and Automation, Milano). "Esperienze di documenttazione meccanica in campo giuridico." *La Ricerca Scientifica,* v. 3, no. 11-12, 1963. p. 293-316.

16. MEYNEN, E., *Documentatio Geographica.* Institut für Landeskunde, Bad Godesberg, 1966-

17. MÖLGAARD-HANSEN, R. and RIGBY, M., eds. *Proceedings of First Seminar on UDC in a Mechanized Retrieval System,* conducted by R. R. Freeman and P. Atherton, Copenhagen, 2-6 Sept. 1968. Copenhagen, Danish Center for Documentation, 1969. (FID/CR report no. 9) (FID 405)

18. SCHNEIDER, K. and KOCH, K. H. *The Use of the UDC in the Production of Mechanized Indexes.* Berlin, Beuth Verlag, 1970. (ZMD-A-21) (English version of no. 12)

19. LIPETZ, B.-A. and SONG, C.T. "How Many Cards Per File Guide?" *Journal American Society for Information Science,* v. 21, no. 2, 1970. p. 140-141.

DISCUSSION

Mr. *Austin* queried Mr. Rigby's diagram showing the relationship between the number of documents in a collection and the number of terms in the indexing language, pointing out that at BNB it had been found that as the number of documents increased there was a gradual decrease in the number of terms added to the thesaurus.

Mr. *Rigby* replied that he also had, at one time, assumed that this would be the case in his own field. However, instead of the expected asymptotic increase levelling off at about 5,000 terms, there had been, at times, a more than linear increase due to the International Geophysical Year activities which had introduced hundreds of new concepts. This was a situation totally different from that of a national bibliography which dealt principally with books.

Mr. *Soergel* commented that decisions about using UDC in mechanized systems ought to be made on the basis of whether or not UDC would do what machines could do with perhaps another scheme. He did not think that UDC displayed enough of the conceptual structure of subject fields which could be revealed by careful analysis.

Mr. *Freeman* said that one possible reply to this was that what finds its way into machine-readable form will often be used as a basis for machine searching.

Mr. *Rigby* commented that the Russians were developing the area of the interface between data retrieval and literature retrieval and that UDC was being used as a switching language in the sense of switching in high-speed computer-to-computer transmission systems which exist already for the World Weather Watch system.

LIBRARY OF CONGRESS SUBJECT HEADINGS — REVIEW AND FORECAST

RICHARD S. ANGELL

Technical Processes Research Office
Library of Congress

A description of the Library of Congress list of subject headings is followed by an indication of the bibliographical records and services in which it is employed. Recommendations for review and improvement of the list are offered within the framework of certain general assumptions and enumerated under six commonly identified problems of the alphabetical subject catalog: Terminology, Specificity, Form and structure of headings, Reference provisions, Complexity and size, and Maintenance. A technique for adopting revised headings within the constraints of the present card catalogs is illustrated and suggestions offered for fuller publication of the total LC subject heading system in future editions.

Note

In the preparation of this paper the author has had the benefit of the advice and assistance of Library of Congress colleagues. The views expressed, however, are his own. Some have the status of recommendations for the review, analysis, and future development of the Library's Subject Heading List. The paper has been cleared in the Library for presentation in this symposium, but no decision has been made on the extent, if any, to which the recommendations will be put into effect.

Introduction

The principal means of subject access to the collections of libraries in the United States is the subject-entry component of the dictionary catalog. For the most part, the subject headings used in these catalogs derive from statements of "objects" and "means" formulated by Charles Ammi Cutter in his *Rules for a Dictionary Catalog*. (1)

The final formulation of Cutter's objectives and rules was taking place at the same time that the Library of Congress was expanding and reorganizing the collections at the turn of the century. His work had a considerable influence on the founders of the Library of Congress catalog. While the early officers were in accord with Cutter and the majority of United States libraries in rejecting the classified or alphabetico-classed catalog in favor of the dictionary catalog, they were unwilling to contemplate the dispersion of headings that could follow from full adherence

143

to Cutter's rule of specific entry, at least in its application to compound headings. They preferred to combine elements of a dictionary and a classified arrangement. The fact that the Library's subject headings began as a mixed system opened the door to inconsistent decisions as the catalog grew.

Another historical circumstance affecting the development of the list is the pattern of organization of subject heading work in the first decades of the century. It was not until 1941 with the establishment of the Subject Cataloging Division that classification and the assignment of subject headings were combined under one technical and administrative direction. Formerly the Catalog Division was responsible for descriptive cataloging and the assignment of subject headings, and the Classification Division for the development and application of the LC schedules. This disposition of responsibilities resulted in some subject heading work being done by non-specialists and led to a rather generalized approach in the assignment and development of subject headings, of which evidences are still found on entries and in the list.

DESCRIPTION OF *LCSH*

A thorough exposition of the Library's subject heading principles and practice would manifestly carry us beyond the proper limits of this paper. For those not already acquainted with the list the most useful exposition is contained in *Subject Headings, a Practical Guide* (2) by David J. Haykin, first chief of the Subject Cataloging Division under the reorganization referred to above. The introduction to the latest edition is also relevant (3). For purposes of completeness in this document, however, and as a point of reference for later discussion, some basic facts about the list should be set forth.

The Library's list of subject headings (hereafter sometimes referred to as LCSH) is a member of the class of controlled pre-coordinate indexing vocabularies. Headings proper have the grammatical form of noun or phrase, the principal types of the latter being adjective-noun, phrases containing a preposition, and phrases containing a conjunction. Phrases may be in normal direct order of words, or inverted.

Headings are amplified as required by 1) the parenthetical qualifier, used principally to name the domain of a single noun for the purpose of resolving homographs; and 2) the subdivision, of which there are four kinds: topic, place, time, and form. References are provided between related headings and from terms not used as headings.

The complete vocabulary of headings and references exists only in the subject portion of the Library's Official Catalog. The published list, as set forth in the Introduction to the 7th edition (3), omits a number of categories of headings. Besides names of persons, families, and corporate bodies, some of the principal omitted categories are: chemical compounds; natural features; structures; metropolitan areas and their features; places and regions, except when needed to show subdivisions; and systematic names of families, genera, and species in botany and zoology.

An entry in the published list is either a heading or a *see* reference to a heading from an expression not used. Under each heading are shown the references from it to other headings and a record, or "tracing," of references made to the heading from other entries. The entry for a heading may also contain one or more of the following features: an indication that it is to be subdivided by place, and in what manner ("direct" or "indirect"); a class number from the LC classification (for some 8 to 10 percent of the headings); and a scope note, specifying the field of application of the heading or any special sense in which it is used. The entry includes a list of subdivisions used with the heading.

The 7th edition of the list and its supplements have been computer-produced from magnetic tape. A consolidated tape of the 7th edition and the first supplement (July 1964-December 1965) is available.

The following auxiliary records are maintained in order to promote uniformity in formulation and usage and to make possible revisions of headings and subdivisions:

1. A file of subdivisions (except form subdivisions) indicating all main headings under which each subdivision has been used.

2. A list of the terms used as qualifiers with a list of the headings after which they appear.

3. A list of the adjectives in adjective-noun phrases which have been entered in the list as inversions, e.g., Art, Primitive.

4. A list of conjunctions and prepositions subarranged by the phrase headings in which they appear, e.g.,
   Kings *and* rulers
   Music *and* war.

5. A record of the scientific headings not included in the published list.

6. A list of geographic names used as main headings or subdivisions.

USES OF *LCSH*

The subject headings have been applied to the Library's collection of more than 4.6 million titles, which is without limit as to subject field and language. The entries form the subject part of two card catalogs in the Library: the Main Catalog, primarily for use by the general public and the reference staff; and the Official Catalog, primarily for the staff of the Processing Department. These catalogs contain, respectively, approximately 15 and 17 million entries, of which an estimated 6 million in each catalog are topical subject entries. In the present fiscal year some 285,000 subject entries will be filed in each catalog for 228,000 currently cataloged titles. Since April of 1968 the Official Catalog has been a divided catalog; that is, it is separated into two sections, name-title and topical subject. Many special divisional catalogs are also maintained, among them those for music and maps. In the *Library of Congress Catalog Books - Subjects,* published since 1950, LC printed cards are displayed under the subject headings assigned to each entry.

In addition to the Library's internal use of the list in its catalogs, other libraries and agencies use it in whole or in part in their subject catalogs and services.

As many have pointed out, and some have deplored, the Library of Congress printed card service carries LC subject headings into the libraries of some 25,000 card subscribers in the United States and 1,200 in other countries. It can be assumed that a certain number of these libraries use the subject headings in their catalogs—often, no doubt, with modification.

A notable example of the subject bibliographies based on LCSH is the *Subject Guide to Books in Print* published annually by the R. R. Bowker Company in New York. The 1970 volume lists 225,000 books under 41,500 headings and includes 49,000 references. LC headings appear in such current lists as the weekly record of current U. S. book publication in *Publisher's Weekly.*

The indexing services of the H. W. Wilson Company use LCSH in one or two cases, and for most others the *Sears' List of Subject Headings* (4) which is very largely derived from LC's. The Sears' list is used for entries in the company's card distribution service.

The presence of LC subject headings on MARC tapes carries them into the new domain of machine-readable bibliographical records. Coverage of English language monographs in the 1969 and later card series is now complete and as of April 30, 1971, the total number of entries included was 130,000. Forty-six libraries and commercial processing services are now subscribers to the MARC tape distribution service. Regional and state networks are among those using the tapes. The Library exchanges its MARC tapes with those of the *British National Bibliography's (BNB)* MARC service. For titles cataloged by *BNB* before receipt of an LC entry, *BNB* assigns LC subject headings to entries appearing on its tapes.

Need for Review

This factual description of LCSH, besides furnishing an inventory of the parts of the system, is intended to convey the size and extent of the bibliographical enterprises of which it is a part. The enormous size of the Library's catalogs, the magnitude of the current cataloging effort as evidenced in the rate of growth of the catalogs, the wide-spread use of the subject heading list, are all impressive, perhaps, in quantitative terms. Unfortunately, in the course of the seven decades in which the Library's catalogs and subject heading list have been growing, certain inconsistencies and anomalies have developed. It would be difficult to imagine a contrary condition, unless perhaps the Library had disposed at every point in time the resources adequate for the necessary continuous revision to reflect changes in usage, semantic shift, abandonment of earlier orthography, and other vagaries of the language. These inconsistencies and anomalies have not escaped the attention of critics, some of whom object to the scheme itself. It would be well, therefore, to take a general look at the status of our subject headings.

In order to lay the basis for a comprehensive review of the Library's subject heading list, I have prepared and submitted to Library officers an outline entitled, "Library of Congress Subject Headings— Problems and Prospects," with the subtitle, "An agenda for analysis and consideration of current criticisms and acknowledged defects." The principal parts of this outline are the following: Uses and purposes of the list, Criteria for judging the list, Criticisms of the list (a synopsis of observations from the literature, experience of LC officers, etc.), Consideration of the criticisms in relation to our criteria, Decision on future course for the list. The last two sections of the outline contain sets of alternatives. The criticisms are to be sorted into valid and invalid; the valid into remediable and irremediable. The decision on future course is divided between Abandon and Maintain. If the former, abandon in favor of . . . (the alternatives are to be supplied); if to maintain, there would follow a program for remedial actions.

GENERAL CONSIDERATIONS

If the suggestions implicit in the foregoing are adopted, a review of LCSH would proceed without preconceptions as to its future. While open-mindedness can be advocated in technical matters, certain general considerations should be borne in mind for their relevance to the ultimate decisions. They do not all point in the same direction.

In considering the future of the list, it seems a reasonable assumption that, as the Library moves toward a machine-readable bibliographic store, we will continue to maintain for an indefinitely long time card catalogs for the use of public and staff, and that this will be true for an even longer period for many of the libraries and other agencies using our bibliographic services. Accordingly, a set of considerations arises from the need to take account of the effect on existing catalogs and services of any changes we might make. For example, if we should decide to use coordinate indexing for certain categories of material we would still have to continue present techniques for the benefit of card subscribers who will still be using conventional displays of subject information.

We also need to be mindful of the objective of compatibility and convertibility with other indexing vocabularies, in particular with the subject authority lists of the National Library of Medicine and the National Agricultural Library.

We should also have in mind the developments toward a switching or intermediary language that would make possible the exchange of bibliographic information between agencies through a single medium. (5)

There is one approach to the review and analysis of LCSH that would seriously impede progress, in my opinion. This would be the assumption that the subject component of the Library's card catalogs is to remain open-ended for the indefinite future. If we accepted this constraint, it would be manifestly impossible to adopt a different system of subject cataloging. Nor, in my opinion, could we make the present system (and therefore the catalogs) materially better unless we can study LCSH as if we were revising it for a new subject catalog. I am persuaded that the Library's list of subject headings can become and remain an up-to-date and responsive instrument for subject access to the collections only if it is developed and maintained under conditions which permit the adoption of changes without the necessity of complete revision of earlier cataloging. Such conditions would be largely provided either by setting a cut-off date for the addition of subject entries to the present card catalogs and starting a new subject catalog at periodic intervals, of a span to be agreed on, or by developing techniques for the introduction of subject heading changes and additions without revision of existing entries. Both alternatives are under study in the Library.

TOPICS FOR REVIEW

The analytic review of LCSH proposed in the foregoing observations might well choose as technical topics the problems enumerated by Frarey in his review of the state of the art of subject headings and the subject catalog. They are: Terminology, Specific entry, Form and structure, Reference apparatus, Complexity and size, and Maintenance. (6) The remarks which follow under these topics contain both exposition and recommendations, expressed or implied.

Terminology

Common usage as the basis for the selection of indexing terms is advocated in American practice. In the absence of evidence to the contrary, it seems a reasonable hypothesis that this basis offers the best chance of maximum correspondence between the prescriptions of indexers and searchers.

A corollary of this principle in the practice of the Library of Congress is that new headings have to be "established." We require evidence that the term or phrase for a new topic has some acceptance in the authoritative current journals and monographs in its field. This enables us to avoid coined terms that do not gain general acceptance, jargon, and other transitory expressions. This policy has its problems and its critics, some of whom have not understood it fully. Although I consider the policy sound, it should be reconsidered in the course of any such general examination as that suggested.

In the present list itself, an obvious element in a thorough revision would be the change from obsolete to current forms. Some of these cases are matters of orthography, e.g., Aeroplanes has become Airplanes; some are dictated by changes in usage, e.g., European War, 1914-1918, to World War, 1914-1918.

Specificity

As a topic in the theory and practice of the alphabetic subject catalog, specificity has proved a difficult attribute to define. For Cutter specific entry meant above all "*not* class entry." We shall see that his antipathy to the latter affected his prescriptions on the formulation of headings.

Some time ago Lilley called attention to the relative nature of the concept (7), and Frarey finds evidence that "the relativity of the principle of specific entry is the major source of difficulty in either its application or its comprehension." (8)

Dunkin observes that "In the discussion of subject headings, 'specific' is often used as if it meant 'narrow' (in contrast with 'broad' or 'general') subjects." (9) He correctly points out that "A specific entry is sometimes for a broad subject, sometimes for a narrow subject." (10) This view is implicit in Haykin's prescription under specificity, "The heading should be as specific as the topic it is intended to cover." (11) He allows, however, that, rather than use a heading broader than the topic, "the cataloger should use two specific headings which will approximately cover it." (12)

For a representative British view of this question we can adduce the following observation by Jack Mills: "Normal British indexing practice . . . is to use for the index description of a document a class which is a summarization of the overall theme of the document. It does not attempt to embrace explicitly the detailed contents of the document . . . The summarization is, however, 'specific' . . . The practice might be called 'single entry specific'." Mills' example is a document on the bacterial diseases of grain crops in storage. The summarization would convey "just this and not something less specific." (13) Mills goes on to characterize American practice as tending "to reject the aim of specific description in a single index heading." (14) He notes some advantages and disadvantages of each method. (The fact that these remarks are made in a paper on classification does not lessen the force of their application to subject headings).

These observations suggest perhaps that we could more usefully deal with the problem of specificity if we substituted for "specific" the notion of "expressive." In this sense specificity is not an attribute of a subject access vocabulary as such (i.e., of its terms) but is rather a function of the total resources of the indexing system, and of the way in which it is used.

In order to achieve expressiveness, American library practice, as exemplified in the list and practices of the Library of Congress, relies in considerable part on the resources of the English language. It uses natural language as naturally as possible. This accounts for the presence in the list of a variety of standard phrase forms, in which relationships between terms are made clear by the syntax of the language. In this respect the principle of common usage, which governs the choice of single terms, is also invoked.

Qualification

Use of the parenthetical qualifier, principally for the resolution of homographs, has been mentioned. LCSH has been criticized for using marks of punctuation, including this one, for more than one purpose.(15) Since it is not a characteristic of English usage that each punctuation sign be used in only one way, it does not seem a reasonable demand to make of an indexing vocabulary. It is proper to expect, however, that in any particular set or complex of headings the parenthesis, for example, be used with a consistent meaning. From this point of view our use of parentheses in headings for cook books, e.g., Cookery (Beef), Cookery (Garnishes), and many others; and for musical compositions, e.g., Concertos (Violin), Sonatas (Flute and piano), etc., is proper in both cases but inconsistent in the first. The use of all marks of punctuation should be scrutinized from this point of view.

Subdivision

It is evident, however, that the limits of expressiveness and precision in index characterizations of document content can not be achieved only by the assignment of single words, by phrases in common use, and by others constructed on the models of common usage. And so, in Haykin's words, "Subdivision . . . is resorted to when no invariable, commonly used and accepted phrase is available with which to express the intended limitation of a subject." (16) However, following Cutter in rejection of the alphabetico-classed heading, he urges, "Subdivision should as far as possible be limited to the form in which the subject matter is presented and the place and time to which it is limited." (17)

Topic. The attempt to exclude subdivision by topic or aspect in Library of Congress practice was never wholly successful. In the absence of a phrase sanctioned by usage, the topical subdivision is allowed by Haykin; for example, SOCIAL PSYCHOLOGY—RESEARCH. He also allows that the topical subdivision may be used in certain cases for uniformity of treatment under a subject, e.g., HEART—DISEASES. (18)

Forms like the following are now used:

AUTOMOBILES—MOTORS—BEARINGS

—. . .

—VALVES

Place. Subdivision by place is used only with headings for which it is indicated in the authority file and the list. Two styles are used: Direct and Indirect. The meaning and application of these signals is explained in the introduction to the 7th edition of the list. (3) The difference can be generally illustrated by these examples:

Direct: BANKS AND BANKING—CLEVELAND

Indirect: MUSIC—SWITZERLAND—ZURICH

At one time a criterion for designating a new heading for place subdivision was the likelihood that large files would accumulate under the heading. This is no longer the case; the sole criterion is suitability of this qualification to the literature of the subject. It may be of interest to note here that the geographic code developed as part of the MARC format has a built-in hierarchy, with the result that all subject headings in our machine-readable records to which this code has been assigned are in effect divided "Indirect."

Period. Time divisions under the history of a country express the periods into which its history is commonly divided. Sometimes a period is denoted by a name, sometimes by a century or other span of dates. The list should be reviewed to express all historical period subdivisions by dates or centuries, followed as appropriate by the period's name. One could say that we have operated on the assumption, for example, that filers in the Library of Congress catalogs could convert U.S.—HISTORY—CIVIL WAR into U.S.—HISTORY—1860-65. This assumption is no longer tenable. The same observations apply to time divisions under headings for literature, art, and other headings, chiefly in the humanities.

Form. Review of the Library's form subdivisions is well under way. A working group of the U. S. National Libraries Task Force on Automation and other Cooperative Activities, consisting of representatives of the Library of Congress, the National Agricultural Library, and the National Library of Medicine, has reviewed a composite list of form subdivisions used with the subject headings of each library. The group will soon be able to recommend adoption of a single list for use by all three libraries. Each subheading will have a scope note stating the appropriate field of application and examples of typical usage. In this review, almost all of the subheadings in the Library of Congress list consisting of terms in series, e.g., "Cartoons, satire, etc.," "Quotations, maxims, etc." would be eliminated by the adoption of the standard list.

Language of text. Although not part of our present practice, I believe that provision for this designation as a part of subject subdivision should be made. Again, the MARC format provides this search capability by including a fixed field for the language or languages of the text.

Complex Subjects

Expression of complex subjects often requires the assignment of more than one heading. We can identify, and should distinguish, two kinds of cases: 1) the multi-topic work and 2) the multi-element work. The assignment of two or more headings for the former is common practice in all systems, to the best of my knowledge. It has to be distinguished, of course, from analytical subject indexing of a work's contents. The difference, to be sure, is not easy to define or to maintain in operational terms.

The expression "multi-element work" is intended to characterize the kind of document, common in technical fields, which is on a narrow topic — "specific" in that sense — and that can only be fully expressed by the representation of all of its elements. This kind of document is not new, but in the post-war period its number, both absolutely and in proportion to the total range of library materials, has greatly increased.

A pre-coordinate system like LCSH has often dealt with this kind of document by the assignment of a heading to each of its elements, for example:

> *Title:* The phenology and growth habits of pines in Hawaii. 1966, 25 pages
>
> *Headings:* 1. Pine—Hawaii
> 2. Phenology
> 3. Trees—Growth

The objection to this kind of treatment is not that the entry under any one of the headings is inaccurate, but that the unmodified heading for Phenology, for example, should be reserved for general works. The consequence is that entries under Phenology have to be "sorted through" to find documents with the limitations of this one. Moreover, we can assume that in most searches the practice entails the unnecessary examination of this entry and its rejection as unlikely to have any material of substance on Phenology in general.

According to the "single-entry specific" practice, the heading for this example would presumably be

PINE—GROWTH—HAWAII

The systematic introduction of this kind of heading would have several consequences. The incidence of the alphabetico-classed form of heading would be increased. The "distributed relative" problem, for which we often use the illustrative *see* or *see also* reference (e.g., "STORAGE *See* . . . subdivision Storage under names of stored products, e.g. . . . . FARM PRODUCTS—STORAGE") would require systematic attention. Most of the solutions have been developed for and used in indexes to classified catalogs and bibliographies. Among them are: cross reference for each element after the first, chain index to a classification schedule, and rotation or selective permutation of the elements of the index string.

Form and structure of headings

In a pre-coordinate indexing system the form of the heading is affected by two factors: 1) the means of making the heading expressive; 2) the choice of lead term. In the foregoing observations on specificity we have dealt with some of the problems and alternatives of the first. The second, choice of lead term, can be dealt with under the heading of form.

Cutter's attempt to avoid inversion as much as possible (his rule on this point is avowedly equivocal) can not be considered an aspect of specificity regarded as expressiveness. If inversion is possible in the grammar of the language, it is surely as expressive as the direct form, e.g., Pheasant, Ring-necked instead of Ring-necked pheasant. Cutter avoided inversion because he regarded it as logically a classed entry. To be sure, it is so in the sense that it groups entries for works on aspects or subtopics of a subject with those for works on the subject as a whole. But surely the inverted adjective-noun phrase is a far cry from the lengthy taxonomic string which he was chiefly aiming to extirpate from library catalogs in the United States.

If establishment of criteria for inversion of phrase headings is a problem in the alphabetical subject catalog, it must be because experience or intuition or both have told us that a single rule is not acceptable, either for direct form always or inverted form always.

A rule that all such headings should be inverted runs at once into unacceptable results. Cutter offers a representative list, beginning with ALIMENTARY CANAL, of headings whose inversions would put them where no one would expect to find them. (19) On the other hand, a fisherman no doubt has a plausible case against a set of headings such as BASS, BLACK BASS, SMALL-MOUTH BASS even if we assume *see also* references from BASS to the last two and *see* references to them from the inversions. The case for using inversion in an example like this lies in the assumption that the searcher would prefer this collocation of entries to the dispersion of the direct forms.

The treatment of this problem by several authorities is reviewed by Dunkin. (20) As he implicitly concludes, attempts to solve the inversion problem by adoption of the "noun rule" result in constructions which sacrifice intelligibility to form and order. A possible test for avoiding unacceptable inversions might be to ask the question: If the second term were used without the first, would the result be accurate, even if imprecise? If the answer is No, the inversion is unacceptable. This gives us ALIMENTARY CANAL without difficulty, and also many phrases beginning with a proper adjective, e.g., BROWNIAN MOVEMENT. Using this question as a test would furnish a ready means of determining whether or not the modifying adjective or noun has removed the generic character of the substantive. If it has, we do not want to invert. If it has not, we may still prefer inversion. In LC practice at least, inversion of most phrases beginning with a linguistic, ethnic, or geographical adjective, or one denoting an historical period is well established, e.g., ART, FRENCH; ARCHITECTURE, MEDIEVAL. But there are exceptions and firmer criteria are needed.

Reference Provisions

In common with many other controlled indexing vocabularies, the LCSH reference structure consists of *see* references from terms not used to headings that are used, and *see also* references from a heading to one of lower rank, and between headings related other than hierarchically. This pattern is diagrammed in Figure 1 and explained in the following statement.

Figure 1 is designed to furnish a graphic display of the basic reference structure of the Library of Congress subject heading list and to suggest the systematic set of considerations associated with the adoption of a new heading or the review of an existing one. The following exposition summarizes current practice; that is, it describes the basis for development and revision of the vocabulary, not the published list of headings. For the purpose of this display, the expression "Central Topic" has been used to identify the term under consideration. Its relationships to other entries in the list are shown in the other boxes:

Broader topic. If the central topic is on a lower level in a hierarchy or is a part of a larger subject, a *see also* reference is made from the broader topic. This is the "downward *see also*" reference and is made from the next higher level only. ("Hierarchy" is used in a general sense, to include not only relations of genus—species but also class—member, topic—subtopic, activity—example, etc.)

Narrower topic. If the central topic is itself a broader topic to another, the downward *see also* reference is made, but only to a topic at the next lower level.

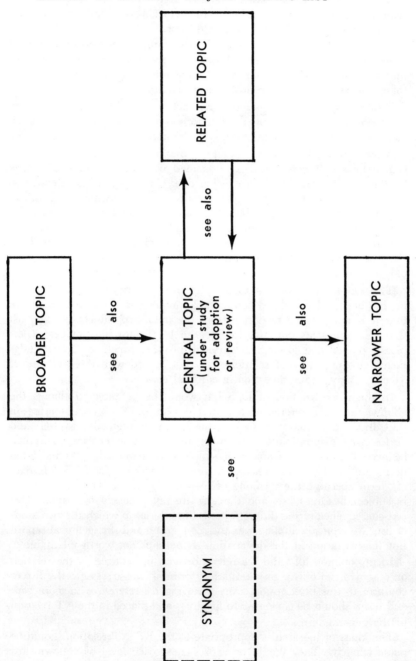

FIGURE 1.

PATTERN OF CROSS-REFERENCE PROVISIONS IN THE
LIBRARY OF CONGRESS SUBJECT HEADING LIST

Related topic. If the central topic is related to another topic but the relationship is coordinate rather than hierarchical, a *see also* reference is made both from and to the central topic.

Synonym. For the purposes of the diagram, this single term is used to comprehend also the *see* reference from antonyms and alternative forms. The dotted box lines are intended to emphasize the fact that these entries in the list are not subject headings.

While only a single box is shown for each relationship, the full diagram for a central term may show more than one relationship of any one kind. Conversely, all of the relationships would not appear in every diagram.

Attention is called to the statement that this diagram represents the systematic set of considerations associated with the adoption of a new heading or the review of an existing one. The diagram is intended to demonstrate the following points: the list does indeed have a classificatory base, though not one directly related to a classification schedule; the *see also* hierarchical references are made in downward direction only and from one level to the next lower level only; related headings have reciprocal references; and *see* references are made in a lateral direction only and not to headings at a higher hierarchical level.

This systematic approach to the integration of new headings into the list has been followed for a considerable number of years. We are aware that it is not possible to derive from the published subject heading list that this represents our practice because 1) the list has not been completely revised and so contains survivals of other practices; 2) our judgments on the nature of relations may not accord with those of others; 3) errors may escape detection in editorial review.

In the reconstruction of LCSH it would be desirable to change the abbreviations for references and tracings to those in common use in thesauri, in the interest of making the list more intelligible to users and of fostering compatibility with other indexing vocabularies. This can be accomplished by means of a simple conversion table, as indicated in Figure 2. There are reasons to prefer "heading" for LCSH instead of "term" because the meaning of hierarchical and collateral references in subject headings lists and thesauri are not precisely the same. This is a consequence of the different kinds of material to which the two kinds of lists are typically applied, i.e., the monograph and the technical report. But this variation in the designations is perhaps not worth maintaining.

In my opinion all valid *see* references can be reduced to the relation of synonym, antonym, or alternative form. I would review the list to conform to this prescription. Any surviving *see* references to more general terms should be converted to headings and placed in the NT relation to the general term.

The kinds of hierarchies appropriate to the BT/NT relation should be made explicit. They should be expressed at each level by a downward *see also* (NT) reference to the term at the next lower level only. References not meeting this specification should be removed.

The BT designation supplies in acceptable form the "upward *see also*" advocated by many writers. Expressed as *"see also"* this reference is incorrect, in my opinion, except in Margaret Mann's formulation of a general reference information card, her example being:

FIGURE 2.

CONVERSION TABLE FOR TYPICAL SUBJECT HEADING
AND THESAURUS REFERENCE DESIGNATIONS

	LCSH		Thesauri	
	Reference	Tracing	Reference	Reciprocal
From unused terms to valid terms	see	x	USE	UF
Between valid terms				
General to specific	sa	xx	NT	BT
Specific to general	[1]		BT	NT
Collateral	sa[2]	xx[2]	RT	RT

1. Not made as such, but the xx tracing of the general-to-specific maintains the connection.
2. When this reference is made and traced in both directions.

BT Broader term
NT Narrower term
RT Related term
sa see also
UF Use for

GLACIERS

Chapters on this subject will often be found in the books entered in this catalog under the heading Geology. (21)

The collateral "see also" reference (RT). It seems likely that anyone who has undertaken a comparison of the provisions for related terms in subject heading lists and thesauri would agree that this is an element of indexing vocabulary construction that deserves careful study. The obesrvations in general thesaurus guidelines and in prefaces to thesauri themselves contain for the most part only the most general kind of prescription for their use. *Thesaurofacet* (22) is an exception: 9 categories of related terms are suggested and illustrated.

Since the related term reference is avowedly suggestive and without precision, it might be considered unnecessary to subject it to rigorous analysis. In my opinion, however, this is not the proper view. Coates has observed that, in the absence of definition of what collateral subjects are, "the collateral relationship may be invoked to justify indiscriminate reference linkages." (23) His suggestion that it be considered "restricted to terms which lie within the same facet of a given generic subject" (24) has been adopted, perhaps independently, in the *Information Retrieval Thesaurus of Education Terms* (25) in which most RT references consist of the number of a subfacet in the thesaurus' faceted array where the subfacet terms are listed.

In its examination of this feature of LCSH the Library now has a valuable resource in a computer program which converts our term relation designations to the set commonly used in thesauri as shown in the conversion table of Figure 2. It has been used to print out certain blocks of headings in LCSH to facilitate comparison with those in the same section of the alphabet in the National Agricultural Library's vocabulary. (26) A printout of the complete tape would greatly facilitate review of the entire reference structure of LCSH. In particular, many NT tracings would be recognized as "one-way collateral *see also's*" and removed or made reciprocal as the case required.

Complexity and Size. Maintenance

The dimensions of Frarey's last two problems as they affect the Library of Congress subject heading list have perhaps been suggested in the earlier account of the size of the catalogs and their rate of growth. The problems can be illustrated by reference to the earlier suggestion that one of the conditions that would make it possible to keep the subject heading list up to date would be the development of techniques for introducing changes without the necessity of complete revision of earlier cataloging. In a study of this problem the Technical Processes Research Office and the Subject Cataloging Division have identified seven principal problems in maintaining currency and accuracy of subject entries in the LC catalogs.

1. Headings originally incorrect
2. Headings which have become incorrect through
   a. change of spelling
   b. change of usage
3. Headings which have become imprecise
4. Headings which have been used imprecisely
5. Invalid two-topic headings: "A and B"
6. Deficiencies resulting from faulty references
7. Problems of long files

Exposition of the details of this study would be inappropriate in this paper, but an illustrative case and an indication of the general nature of the proposed solutions may be of interest.

The problem chosen for illustration is "Deficiencies resulting from faulty references." An example can be found under EROSION on page 441 of the 7th edition of the subject heading list. (3) While there are *see also* references to such headings as BEACH EROSION, DUST STORMS, and RUN-OFF among others, SOIL EROSION is a *see* reference to EROSION. This anomaly was corrected in August of 1968, but until then the consequence of the reference provisions was that entries for SOIL EROSION had to be found in the file of general works under EROSION. Moreover, this incorrect reference resulted in an indirect connection between SOIL EROSION and SOIL CONSERVATION.

The following statement suggests the general nature of the solutions proposed by the study, namely, information cards filed with the affected entries and a prescription for the changes to be made in references:

Information cards

SOIL EROSION

Here are entered works on soil erosion cataloged after September 1, 1968. Works on this topic cataloged before this date will be found among those entered under Erosion.

EROSION

Use of this heading for works on soil erosion was discontinued on August 31, 1968. Works on soil erosion cataloged after this date are entered under Soil erosion.

References

Cancel   Erosion
              sa Soil conservation
                    Soils
          Soil erosion see Erosion

Add   Erosion
              sa Soil erosion
          Soil conservation
              sa Soil erosion
          Soil erosion
              sa Soil conservation

The study recognized that the examples of this possible technique could not provide a demonstration of its effect on the texture of the catalog, but accepted it as self-evident that a vastly more complex reference structure would be adverse to ready catalog consultation by users. The importance of communicating any such changes to card subscribers so that they could adopt or reject our solution was also recognized. Let me make it clear that these procedures have only been offered for consideration and have not been put into effect for any heading. The SOIL EROSION case has been taken care of in our catalogs by changing the affected entries and references. It is therefore a hypothetical example of how it might have been dealt with.

Publication of Future Editions of LCSH

In conclusion I should like to make some comments and suggestions on the content of future editions of the published list. They arise from a belief in the importance of making the list and its appurtenant records available as fully as possible to the users of the Library's bibliographical services and all others having an interest in the list. As the topics of recorded discourse multiply and as collections consequently grow in size and diversity, it becomes more and more important that the first step in the effort to find relevant materials by subject should be to examine the vocabulary of the indexing language. It follows that in more and more searches it will be economical to make them in two stages: first in the vocabulary and then in the catalog or display of subject entries.

The following outline suggests the sections into which future editions of LCSH might be organized:

Section 1   *Description, Conventions, Rules*
      2   *Alphabetical list of headings, including*
          see and see-also references
      3   *Subdivisions*
          Form (generally applicable)
          Topic, each with headings under which it is used
          Period, as used under names of places
      4   *Keyword list of headings and subdivisions*
      5   *Musical compositions*

A few observations on some of the sections may be appropriate.

Section 2 would include subject category designations for each heading in order to make possible the development of automatic techniques for extracting lists in special fields. Use of the main classes and principal subclasses of our schedules is assumed. A heading would have as many category designations as required to place it in each of the special lists of headings in which its membership would be appropriate.

Except for personal and corporate names, names of natural features, and categories of similar character, the headings excluded from the 7th edition and its supplements would be included in future editions. This is important in order that the references associated with the presently excluded headings be available. This is also a necessary basis for the establishment of conversion algorisms with other vocabularies.

The three lists of subdivisions in *Section 3* would include the standard list of forms now being developed, the subdivision control file, and a list of period subdivisions under names of places formerly published separately.

The keyword list proposed for *Section 4* would be a rotated list of headings and subdivisions, in order to provide comprehensive access to terms whenever they occur. Subdivisions would be identified by an arbitrary sign and this would constitute a reference to the list of topical subdivisions in the preceding section. If kept up to date with supplementary files between editions, this list might serve as a substitute for the *see* references now made in the card catalog between alternative forms, since all terms in phrase headings, for example, would be displayed.

The suggestion that headings for musical compositions constitute a separate section derives from the special nature of the materials and the consequent special character of the headings. The headings for music history, criticism, and pedagogy would be contained in the general list of *Section 2*. These headings could be extracted for separate publication, to be used with the composition headings in special music libraries.

Conclusion

The study of the Library's subject heading list suggested in the foregoing review could result in a different system in the course of time. The most reasonable path of progress, however, is considered to be the improvement of the list in its present terms, as suggested under the several topics for review. This course provides the obvious advantages of orderly evolution. It also recognizes the fact that, during the course of its seven decades of growth, the list and the catalogs in which it is embodied have been of substantial service in the library community.

REFERENCES

1. CUTTER, C. A. *Rules for a Dictionary Catalog.* 4th ed. Washington, Government Printing Office, 1904. (First edition, 1876, has title: *Rules for a Printed Dictionary Catalogue.*)

2. HAYKIN, D. J. *Subject Headings; a Practical Guide.* Washington, U. S. Government Printing Office, 1951.

3. LIBRARY OF CONGRESS. *Subject Headings Used in the Dictionary Catalogs of the Library of Congress.* 7th ed. Ed. by M. V. Quattlebaum. Washington, 1966.

4. *Sears' List of Subject Headings.* 9th ed. Ed. by B. M. Westby. New York, The H. W. Wilson Company, 1965.

5. COATES, E. J. "Library Science and Documentation Literature: a New Development in International Co-operation." *Library Association Record,* v. 70, no. 7, 1968, p. 178-179.

    ———————— "Switching Languages for Indexing." *Journal of Documentation,* v. 26, no. 2, 1970, p. 102-110.

6. FRAREY, C. J. "Subject Headings." *In: The State of the Library Art.* Ed. by R. R. Shaw. New Brunswick, Rutgers—The State University, 1960, v. 1, pt. 2.

7. LILLEY, O. L. "How Specific is Specific?" *Journal of Cataloging and Classification,* v. 11, no. 1, 1955, p. 3-8.

8. FRAREY, C. J. *Op. cit.* p. 59.

9. DUNKIN, P. S. *Cataloging U.S.A.* Chicago, American Library Association, 1969, p. 68.

10. *Ibid.*

11. HAYKIN, D. J. *Op. cit.* p. 9.

12. *Ibid.*

13. MILLS, J. "Some Current Problems of Classification for Information Retrieval." *Classification Society Bulletin,* v. 1, no. 4, 1968, p. 24.

14. *Ibid.*

15. DAILY, J. E. "Many Changes, no Alteration." *Library Journal,* v. 92, no. 1967, p. 3962.

16. HAYKIN, D. J. *Op. cit.* p. 27.

17. HAYKIN, D. J. *Loc. cit.*

18. HAYKIN, D. J. *Op. cit.* p. 36.

19. CUTTER, C. A. *Op. cit.* p. 73.

20. DUNKIN, P. S. *Op. cit.* Chapter 5, p. 65-95 *passim.*

21. MANN, M. *Introduction to Cataloging and the Classification of Books.* 2d ed. Chicago, American Library Association, 1943, p. 151.

22. *Thesaurofacet,* a thesaurus and faceted classification for engineering and related subjects. Compiled by J. Aitchison, et al. Whetstone, Leicester, The English Electric Co. Ltd., 1969, p.xviii.

23. COATES, E. J. *Subject Catalogues, Headings and Structure.* London, The Library Association, 1960, p. 73-74.

24. *Ibid.* p. 74.

25. BARHYDT, G. C., et al. *Information Retrieval Thesaurus of Education Terms.* Cleveland, Case Western Reserve University Press, 1968.

26. NATIONAL AGRICULTURAL LIBRARY. *Agricultural/Biological Vocabulary.* 1st ed. Washington, United States Department of Agriculture, 1967, 2 vols. and 1st supplement, 1968.

DISCUSSION

Mr. *Soergel* said that for him the LCSH is a thesaurus and that it would probably be impossible to invent any good definition which would separate the two concepts. He asked why upward "see also" or BT references could not be introduced and also whether or not Mr. Angell considered it feasible and useful to set up a kind of core classification for LCSH such as he had attempted to describe in his paper. The compound headings could then be split up into the elemental concepts of the core classification and one could produce a kind of index to LCSH in terms of those elemental concepts.

Mr. *Angell* replied that he would need to give the latter suggestion further consideration before answering. On the first point he said that he believed that upward "see also" references were not proper in the type of catalog for which LCSH had been designed because if one uses the form "see also" it implies that material will be found there, whereas in a thesaurus the BT formulation had a different kind of meaning for both the indexer and for the searcher. In a dictionary catalog the only correct formulation was that proposed by Margaret Mann, i.e.:

GLACIERS

> Material on this subject is often found
> in works entered under GEOLOGY in
> this catalog.

Mr. *Freeman* asked if it was possible to estimate what percentage of headings required revision.

Mr. *Angell* replied that at this stage it was not possible to give such an estimate. As examples of originally incorrect headings, and headings which had become incorrect through usage, he cited, in the first category:

Latin America *see* SPANISH AMERICA

and, in the second category, the replacement of the term Mohammedan by the now correct term MOSLEM, and Mohammedanism by ISLAM. Mr. *Spalding,* replying to a question on the probability of Mr. Angell's proposals being adopted by the Library of Congress, said that Mr. Welsh, Director of the Processing Department, had suggested two years ago that the Library should close its catalogs (in the sense of beginning a new catalog from a given date) in order to give an opportunity for major changes to be made, not only in subject headings, but also in name headings. This suggestion was still under active discussion within the Library and it was the Processing Department's hope that at least the subject catalog could be closed in order to undertake a thorough overhaul of the subject heading system.

PANEL DISCUSSION

PANELISTS

Dr. Harold Wooster (Moderator) National Library of Medicine
Mr. Robert R. Freeman   National Oceanic and Atmospheric
                                Administration
Dr. Laurence B. Heilprin   School of Library and Information
                                Services, University of Maryland
Mr. J. I. Smith   ERIC Clearinghouse on Library and
                                Information Sciences
Miss Sarah M. Thomas   Environmental Protection Agency
Dr. Isaac D. Welt   American University

This concluding session of the Symposium was organized so as to give each panelist about ten minutes in which to make a contribution. The following is an edited version of the taped transcript.

Dr. *Heilprin* said that he had received some input from the Symposium on two topics: one of them being the economics of classification, the other, the stability of classification schemes. On the former, one of the principal factors was the competition for scarce resources and it seemed obvious that the two principal competitors for the role of international system, namely UDC and LC, differed considerably in respect to two aspects which had significance for this competition, i.e. in the specific and logical, or switching, efficiency in the service rendered for search and retrieval, and in the administrative services involved in keeping the system up to date.

On the stability of classification schemes, he noted that in the conceptual lattices and in the file structures which attempted to reproduce them, it was clear that the most general classes have the greatest stability, whereas the classes lower down the hierarchy change more and more rapidly the deeper one goes. This leads to the conclusion that there is some merit in trying to achieve a world classification system using the first two or three levels which are comparatively stable: it is a matter of determining the threshold in terms of rates of obsolescence in order to decide how specific such a system should attempt to be.

Miss *Thomas* said that in all of the sessions she had attended the speakers were talking about creating tools which information people were going to use. She was convinced, however, that the users (at least of special

164

libraries) do not think about information retrieval in the same way as information scientists. The user thinks of single words which, hopefully, will lead him to the information he needs, and sometimes the retrieval of a single item will lead to others through citations. Mrs. Aitchison had mentioned that she had tried to think in the same way as users in making *Thesaurofacet* and this is certainly the direction in which the makers of indexing languages must go.

Another point which Miss Thomas raised was the possibility, indeed the desirability, of closing the subject catalog to a collection and starting again every few years. She saw no other solution to the problem which Mr. Lloyd had raised when he said that the changing needs of scientists make the control of subject terms extremely difficult. Most systems for changing and updating thesauri and subject heading lists and classification schemes were so cumbersome and so difficult to negotiate that by the time they had changed the words also had changed. It did not seem likely that very large systems for international use could adjust as rapidly as user populations would require.

Mr. *Freeman* began by disputing the statement in the Symposium publicity that we now know enough about the basic requirements of subject retrieval to apply modern principles to large public and national libraries and ultimately to international systems of information retrieval and exchange. An important future trend will be the construction and distribution of larger and far fewer machine-readable date bases. A further trend is that of co-operatively identifying and indexing the raw material for such data bases—in many cases sharing this job on an international basis.

An outcome of these two facts should be a reduction in the emphasis on controlled indexing which ought to be to the eventual benefit of users. This is not to say that work on thesauri should be abandoned but that the use of such tools will be for better lead-in vocabularies, allowing the users to pose questions in whatever terms they wish.

Successful systems will be those which have the better administrative services for production and distribution. In the past, more attention has been paid to technical systems, probably to an undue extent.

Dr. *Welt* said that when he first came across the word "classification" he had thought of it purely in relation to the Aristotelian concept of the classification of knowledge: it had never occurred to him that the word would be associated with shelving books. He pointed out that "natural" classification systems which were truly international languages existed in the biological sciences and that the periodic table in chemistry was also a classification scheme; however, in the social sciences, which were human constructs, it was difficult to imagine the creation of a classification system which could be acceptable to everybody. The only satisfactory course of action in these fields seemed to be to rely purely upon citation indexes.

In relation to shelving, Dr. Welt believed that the distinction between book and journal article was meaningless at a time when the collection-of-readings type of publication was increasing, and that books should be treated as documents and indexed to the same degree as technical reports or articles. Furthermore, the costs of maintaining classified shelf sequences especially in large libraries (which, in any case, were often closed access libraries) were very high, not only from the equipment point of view but also from the aspect of the various functions connected with shelving. He believed that the answer was accession number shelving, coupled with an increase in the use of microfiches.

Mr. *Smith* said that he intended to adopt the role of the devil's advocate and that some of his comments would be due to that role rather than to his personal impressions of the Symposium. He asked why the attendees were present, having been somewhat surprised to discover, from his own investigations, that, although a good part of the Symposium had been devoted to general systems such as LC, only 7% of the people attending were from public libraries, whereas 50% were from special libraries, 21% were from universities, and 22% were from national libraries. Mr. Smith's remaining questions were directed at understanding what the participants were intending to do with any information which they had garnered at the conference; how many were in a position to affect policy in relation to information retrieval; how many were going to create their own thesauri or classification schemes; and why there had been so little discussion, except between the speakers.

GENERAL DISCUSSION

Mr. *Wilson* drew Miss Thomas' attention to D. V. Arnold's dictum that the indexing and information retrieval system in a special library should be renewed every five years because either the needs of the organization, or the nature of the field, or both, will have changed so radically in that time, that the existing system would be archaic.

Mrs. *Sherwood,* in replying to Mr. Smith, said that she had attended the conference as a newcomer to the field in order to find ideas which would be applicable to her situation. She had seen the desirability fo some overall system—a role which perhaps UDC could fill, and also the need for a system for information retrieval rather than document retrieval for the kind of information which her users needed. She felt that perhaps she had received a push in the right direction as a result of attending the Symposium.

Mr. *Price* said that he had attended the Symposium because he enjoyed studying the field of subject retrieval, and that in addition to enjoyment, he had also found a number of useful ideas, for example, the need for a taxonomy of information retrieval languages that M. de Grolier had discussed, and also he now had a better awareness of the problem of a consistent terminology for the field.

M. *de Grolier* said that he regarded meetings of this kind as a sort of stocktaking which needed to be done from time to time, and that this meeting had been particularly useful in being an international stock-taking. He had felt, in retrospect, that the economics of information retrieval systems had been rather neglected, as indeed it was generally neglected. He believed that it was wrong to regard meetings of this kind as necessarily producing information which could be of immediate use in decision making, however, he felt that the Symposium had not been unhelpful in this respect.

LIST OF PARTICIPANTS

Adelman, Jean S.	University Museum, University of Pennsylvania
Anderson, Hattie T.	Applied Physics Laboratory Johns Hopkins University
Anglemyer, Mary	Woodrow Wilson International Center for Scholars, Smithsonian Institute
Anthony, Betty	Institute for Defense Analysis
Askey, Donald E.	National Agricultural Library
Barbalas, Louis X.	National Oceanic and Atmospheric Administration, Lake Survey Center
Bauman, Jr. Frederick W.	Center for Applied Linguistics
Bread, Charles C.	Library of Congress
Bernal, Emilia	Graduate School of Librarianship, Univ. of Puerto Rico
Blume, Edward J.	Library of Congress
Brodney, Kay	Library of Congress
Bruch, Virginia	Army Library, Pentagon
Burris, Ray E.	Health Services and Mental Health Administration
Canick, Maureen L.	ERIC Processing and Reference Facility
Cantrell, Carl W.	National Agricultural Library
Cardin, Clarisse	National Library of Canada
Chandler, Harold R.	D.C. Public Library
Chapman, Elwynda K.	National Oceanic and Atmospheric Administration
Cheek, Madge C.	U.S. Army Environmental Hygiene Agency
Christian, Portia	Academy of Food Marketing
Clarke, Robert F.	National Institutes of Health
Cresswell, Edward P.	Dept. of the Navy
Custer, Benjamin A.	Library of Congress
Dillon, Martin	School of Library Science Univ. of North Carolina
Dunn, Harold E.	James Branch Cabell Library
Fass, Evelyn E.	Institute for Defense Analyses
Feeney, Patricia	Defense Intelligence Agency
Fodor, Beth	Dept. of Interior
Frosio, Eugene T.	Library of Congress
Fuellhart, Patricia	U.S. Bureau of Census
Garman, Leroy	U.S. Army Environmental Hygiene Agency
Gilbert, Marjorie M.	Arlington County Public Library

Goodstein, Sylvia	Montgomery College - Rockville Campus
Harvey, Dixie	Model Cities
	Community Information Center
Hopkins, Isabella	NC News Service, Documentation Center
Jackson, Sidney L.	Kent State University
James, Mary G.	NASA Scientific and
	Technical Information Facility
Jones, Margaret M.	University of Maryland
	Health Sciences Library
Karklins, Vija L.	Smithsonian Institution
King, Charles H.	Smithsonian Institution
Knable II, John P.	Library of Congress
Lendvay, Olga	National Agricultural Library
Lindley, Jane A.	Library of Congress
Listfeldt, Mary	University of Maryland
	Health Sciences Library
Maddox, Bennie F.	Coastal Engineering Research Center
Malley, Patricia	U.S. Army Computer Systems Support
	and Evaluation Command
Meserve, Janet R.	Library of Congress
Miller, Mary Lou	Library of Congress
Olson, Nancy	Mankato State College
Ostrove, Geraldine	Peabody Institute Library
Painter, Ann F.	Graduate School of Library Science,
	Drexel Univ.
Peters, Martha Ann	Enoch Pratt Free Library
Phillips, Delores	School of Library Science,
	University of Toronto
Powell, Myrl D.	Library of Congress
Price, Douglas S.	ERIC Processing and Reference Facility
Pritchett, Morgan	Milton S. Eisenhower Library
	Johns Hopkins University
Rafter, Sharlene G.	Geophysical Sciences Library,
	National Oceanic and
	Atmospheric Administration
Rather, John C.	Library of Congress
Reed, Emily W.	Enoch Pratt Free Library
Reed, Mary Jane	New York State Library
Rupp, Susan K.	Westvaco Corporation
Sanderson, Sue E.	U.S. Army. War College Library
Sawaryn, Radomira M.	Western Electric Co.
Samuel, Parkash	Library of Congress
Schneider, John	National Institutes of Health
Schofer, H. Stanley	Highway Research Board

Scott, Edith	Library of Congress
Sherwood, Gertrude B.	National Bureau of Standards
Shumway, Norman P.	National Library of Medicine
Sims, Barry R.	Coastal Engineering Research Center
Slezak, Eva A.	Enoch Pratt Free Library
Smith, Janet	Institute for Defense Analyses
Smith, Jean Chandler	Smithsonian Institution
Sohn, Berta S.	Smithsonian Institution
Spalding, C. Sumner	Library of Congress
Sundermyer, Ruth	Enoch Pratt Free Library
Tabor, Leonard	National Agricultural Library
Taylor, Louise A.	Milner Library, Illinois State University
Terwilliger, Gloria	Northern Virginia Community College
Tubio, Manuel	Glassboro State College
Wilcox, Margaret A.	World Bank
Wilson, Florence N.	Denver Public Library
Witty, Francis J.	Catholic University
Zenich, Margaret	U.S. Corps of Engineers
Zlatich, Marko	World Bank

RETRIEVAL SYSTEMS USED
BY THE PARTICIPANTS

(from data submitted on application forms)

CLASSIFICATION SYSTEMS

Dewey Decimal	17
Library of Congress	48
UDC	2
National Library of Medicine	1
Own system	2
No classification system	5

ALPHABETICAL LISTS OF TERMS

Sears' list of subject headings	1
LC subject heading list	52
Thesauri	
Agricultural/Biological Vocabulary	2
LEX	3
LINCS*	1
NLM MeSH	1
NASA Thesaurus	1
Pulp and Paper Institute of Canada	1
Thesaurus of ERIC Descriptors	4
Thesaurus of Engineering and Scientific Terms	2
Not specified	4
Own list	11

IR SYSTEMS OPERATION

Manual	37
Mechanized	4
Both	18

*Language Information Network Clearinghouse System

INDEX

Page numbers followed by the letter d indicate a topic referred to in discussion or the name of a discussant. Page numbers followed by the letter r indicate a bibliographical reference. Page numbers followed by an asterisk indicate an illustration.

generic posting 48, 55
generic trees 29, 74, 78*, 79*
Geneva 121
Geo-Sciences Abstracts 139
German National Bibliography 138
Germany 70, 116, 119, 120
Gesner, Konrad 14
Gilchrist, A. 29
Gilyarevskii, R. S. 25r
Gomersall, A. 96r
Goodman, N. 27r
Great Britain *see* United Kingdom
Grolier, E. de 30, 34r, 60d, 61,
125d, 166, 167d
Groupe informatiste de bibliothèques
universitaires et spécialisées
(GIBUS) 138
The Hague 120

Harris, J. L. 11, 26r
Haykin, D. J. 144, 149, 150, 151, 161r
Subject Headings: A Practical Guide
144
Heaps, D. 119, 138
Heilprin, L. B. 164
Herceg-Novi 117
hierarchical displays 77, 83
hierarchical notation 101
hierarchy 37-40, 44-45, 50, 74, 91
definition 37
Hindson, R. 119, 139
history of classifications 30-31
Holmstrom, J. E. 29, 34r
homographs 150
hospitality of notation 88
Hulme, E. W. 28, 34r

ICP *see International Classifica-
tion of Patents*
ICSSD *see* International Council for
Social Sciences Documentation
ICSU see International Council of
Scientific Unions
IRRD *see* International Road Research
Documentation
IRRD Thesaurus 74, 96r
ISO *see* International Organi-
zation for Standardization
Index Medicus 20
indexing 5, 6, 35-59, 62, 65, 108-109
by computers 21-22, 99, 107
specificity 10-11, 22
time 114d
indexing languages *see* information
retrieval languages

information cards 159
information retrieval languages 28-32,
117, 171
compatibility 31, 148
definition 28, 37
efficiency 30, 37
models 31
revision 165d
terminology 29, 32d, 136, 148
typology 29, 32d
universal systems 31
*Information Retrieval Thesaurus of
Education Terms* 158, 162r
Information Service for Physics,
Electrotechnology and Control
(INSPEC) 74, 98
INIS *see* International Nuclear
Information System
INSPEC *see* Information Service for
Physics, Electrotechnology and
Control
Integrated Library Administration
and Cataloguing System [Nether-
lands] 139
integrative levels 67-68
Interdepartmental Committee on At-
mospheric Sciences (ICAS) [U.S.]
139, 141r
intermediate lexicon 70
International Atomic Energy Authority,
74, 97r
*International Classification of
Patents* (ICP) 121
International Council for Social
Sciences Documentation (ICSSD)
121
International Council of Scientific
Unions (ICSU) 117
International Federation for Docu-
mentation *see* Fédération Inter-
nale de Documentation
*International Glossary of Hydro-
logy* 139
International Nuclear Information
Systems (INIS) 74, 76*
International Organization for
Standardization (ISO) 121
International Road Research Document-
ation (IRRD) 74, 96r
INTREX 20, 27r
inverted files 46-47, 49
inverted headings 153-154
Ireland, R. 96r